Glencoe

The Developing Child

Building Brighter Futures

Student Activity Workbook

Glencoe

The McGraw-Hill Companies

Printed in the United States of America

Send all inquiries to:
Glencoe/McGraw-Hill
8787 Orion Place
Columbus, OH 43240-4027

ISBN: 978-0-07-888433-7   (Student Activity Workbook)
MHID: 0-07-888433-0   (Student Activity Workbook)

ISBN: 978-0-07-888434-4   (Student Activity Workbook TAE)
MHID: 0-07-888434-9   (Student Activity Workbook TAE)

8 9 10 HSO 12

Table of Contents

For additional projects and study tools, visit this book's Online Learning Center at glencoe.com.

Table of Contents

Table of Contents

 For additional projects and study tools, visit this book's Online Learning Center at glencoe.com.

Table of Contents

Table of Contents

 For additional projects and study tools, visit this book's Online Learning Center at glencoe.com.

Table of Contents

Table of Contents

 For additional projects and study tools, visit this book's Online Learning Center at glencoe.com.

Table of Contents

For additional projects and study tools, visit this book's Online Learning Center at glencoe.com.

Chapter 1 Learn About Children
Section 1.1 Make a Difference in Children's Lives
 Note Taking

Directions As you read, write notes, facts, and main ideas in the Note Taking column. Write key words and short phrases in the Cues column. Then summarize the section in the Summary box.

Cues	Note Taking
• typical childhood behavior	**BENEFITS OF STUDYING CHILDREN** • Children's behaviors can be fascinating and frustrating.
• stage of life	**VIEWS OF CHILDHOOD** • People look at childhood in different ways.

Summary
By studying children, you can learn why they act the way they do.

Chapter 1 Learn About Children

Section 1.1 Make a Difference in Children's Lives

 English Language Arts
Child Care Careers

NCTE 3 Apply strategies to interpret texts.

Directions Read the paragraphs about careers in child care. Then read the scenarios and suggest in writing the best type of child care worker for each situation. The first one is done for you as an example.

Child Care Careers

There are many ways to make a living providing care for children. You may already be earning extra money by babysitting. Responsible teens who get along well with children and who know what to do in an emergency can make excellent babysitters. Teens can also work as camp counselors during vacations from school. You will need to enjoy working and living with children, and you must be prepared to have little or no time to yourself. You can learn a lot of skills and make a lot of friends as a camp counselor.

Day care providers generally provide all-day care for one or more children in their homes or in a center. Day care providers will usually need to undergo background checks and may need to have a license from the city, county, or state in which they live.

In most states, preschool teachers are required to take some classes in early childhood education. This helps prepare them to help young children learn the skills they will need in kindergarten.

A pediatrician is a medical doctor who takes extra classes to learn specifically about children and how to help them when they are sick or injured. Pediatricians spend many years in school to learn to provide health care for children.

1. Shaun's parents are going to dinner. Who could take care of four-year-old Shaun?
   babysitter
   _____

2. Rihanna will be going to kindergarten next year. Her mom is not sure she is ready for school. Who might she contact?

   _____

3. Anna must go back to work because she has used up her maternity leave. Who should she contact to care for little Carlos?

   _____

4. Lin has come down with a severe case of the flu. Who should her dad contact?

   _____

5. Bobby would like to work with children in a fun atmosphere while he is on summer break from high school. What job might be good for him?

   _____

Chapter 1 Learn About Children
Section 1.1 Make a Difference in Children's Lives

 Study Skills
Reading Strategies

Directions Read the following reading strategies. Then rewrite the headings into questions. You may add your own words to do this. The first one is done for you as an example.

Reading the Text	
Preread	• Think about what you already know. • Read the titles, introduction, heads, and summary for the entire chapter. • Look at the visuals. Read the captions.
Question	• Ask questions as you read each heading. • Change each heading into one or more questions. • Use the words *who*, *what*, *when*, *where*, *why*, and *how*. • Write the questions in your study notebook. • Leave space for the answers.
Read	• Read to find the answers to the questions you asked.
Write	• In your notebook, write the answers under each question.

Benefits of Studying Children

1. What are the benefits of studying children?

Views of Childhood

2. _____

Importance of Childhood Development

3. _____

Stages of Life After Childhood

4. _____

Why Observe Children?

5. _____

How to Observe Young Children

6. _____

Chapter 1 Learn About Children
Section 1.2 Studying Children

 Note Taking

Directions As you read, write notes, facts, and main ideas in the Note Taking column. Write key words and short phrases in the Cues column. Then summarize the section in the Summary box.

Cues	Note Taking
• stimulation	**IMPORTANCE OF CHILDHOOD DEVELOPMENT** • Childhood prepares us for adulthood.
• human life cycle	**STAGES OF LIFE AFTER CHILDHOOD** • Development continues from birth to death in stages that each present challenges.
Summary	

Chapter 1 Learn About Children
Section 1.2 Studying Children

 Social Studies
Applying Behavioral Theories

NCSS IV D Individual Development and Identity Apply concepts, methods, and theories about the study of human growth and development.

Directions Match the theorist and his ideas to the application examples. Put the letter of the theorist in the space provided.

	Theorist	Ideas
a	Sigmund Freud	Personality develops through a series of stages. Experiences in childhood profoundly affect adult life.
b	Jean Piaget	Children go through four stages of learning.
c	Lev Vygotsky	Biological development and cultural experience influence children's ability to learn. Social contact is essential to intellectual development.
d	Erik Erikson	Personality develops in stages. Each stage includes a unique psychological crisis.
e	B.F. Skinner	When a child's actions have positive results, they will be repeated. Negative results will make the actions stop.
f	Albert Bandura	Children learn by imitating others. Although the environment shapes behavior, behavior also affects environment.

___c___ **1.** As three-year-old Jonathan interacted with family members, his language skills improved.

_____ **2.** Susie watched her mother bathe her baby brother, and then Susie bathed her favorite doll.

_____ **3.** Jessie is sure that having been shut in a dark closet by his brother as a young child has contributed to the fact that he is now afraid of the dark.

_____ **4.** Two-year-old Jennifer became frustrated as she tried, but failed, to tie her shoes.

_____ **5.** In high school, Kelly was depressed because she did not seem to fit in any of the social groups on campus.

_____ **6.** Adam's mother smiled and said, "Good boy," when he put away his toy car, so Adam put away all of the rest of his toys, too.

Chapter 1 Learn About Children
Section 1.2 Studying Children

Test Prep
Test-Taking Checklist

Directions Read the tips for preparing for tests. Then take the sample test. Circle the letter next to the phrase that best completes the sentence.

Preparing for Tests
• Organize the notes you took while reading the text and in class. • Set aside time you will need to study for the test. • Test yourself on the material. • Finish studying the day before the exam. Read your notes again before you go to bed. • Get a good night's sleep. • On the day of the test, try to relax, be confident, and do your best.

1. Stimulation:
   a. will cause a baby to fall asleep.
   b. is any activity that arouses a baby's sense of sight, sound, touch, taste, and smell.
   c. has not been found to help young children learn.
   d. allows parents to better understand their child.

2. The five basic areas of child development include:
   a. emotional, financial, social, intellectual, and moral.
   b. educational, spiritual, emotional, social, and physical.
   c. physical, emotional, social, intellectual, and moral.
   d. physical, emotional, social, educational, and moral.

3. Researchers have found that child development:
   a. is similar for each individual.
   b. proceeds at an individual rate.
   c. builds upon earlier learning.
   d. All of the above are true.

4. Self-esteem:
   a. is not involved with people's ability to face and overcome the challenges of each developmental stage.
   b. causes people to feel that they are constantly disappointing others.
   c. is critical to a child's development.
   d. is not related to people's success in life.

5. During the stage of late adulthood:
   a. most adults pursue new careers.
   b. most adults establish their roots.
   c. many adults finish their education.
   d. many adults retire.

Chapter 1 Learn About Children

Section 1.3 Observing Young Children

 Note Taking

Directions As you read, write notes, facts, and main ideas in the Note Taking column. Write key words and short phrases in the Cues column. Then summarize the section in the Summary box.

Cues	Note Taking
• observing children	**WHY OBSERVE CHILDREN?** • We learn more about children by observing them than by reading about them.
• subjective point of view	**HOW TO OBSERVE YOUNG CHILDREN** • There are steps to observing children.

Summary

Through observing children you can learn things you cannot learn from a book.

Chapter 1

Chapter 1 Learn About Children
Section 1.3 Observing Young Children

 Science
Observation Records

NSES A Develop abilities necessary to do scientific inquiry, understandings about scientific inquiry.

Directions For each type of observation record provide a definition and your own original example of when it might be used.

1. Running Record A running record is a record of everything observed for a set period, such as 15 minutes. An observer wants to see a child's social skills.

_____

_____

_____

2. Anecdotal Record _____

_____

_____

_____

3. Frequency Count _____

_____

_____

_____

_____

4. Developmental Checklist _____

_____

_____

_____

_____

Chapter 1 Learn About Children
Chapter Vocabulary

English Language Arts
Matching Definitions

NCTE 12 Use language to accomplish individual purposes.

Chapter 1

Directions Choose the vocabulary term from the list that best matches each definition. Write the word in the right column of the table. Note: You will not use all of the terms.

Content Vocabulary		Academic Vocabulary
• anecdotal record	• heredity	• assumption
• baseline	• human life cycle	• impact
• caregiver	• interpretation	• judgment
• confidentiality	• objective	• moral
• developmental checklist	• running record	• sequence
• developmental task	• self-esteem	• theory
• environment	• stimulation	
• frequency count	• subjective	
	• typical behavior	

Definition	Word
to rely on personal opinions and feelings, rather than facts, to judge an event	subjective
a fact that is taken for granted	
a report of a child's actions that concentrates on a specific behavior or area of development	
any activity that arouses a baby's sense of sight, sound, touch, taste, and smell	
a belief; an abstract thought or idea	
a person who takes care of a child	
a tally of how often a certain behavior occurs	
the biological transfer of certain characteristics from earlier generations	
the people, places, and things that surround and influence a person	
the analysis an observer forms and expresses	
the challenge to be met or skill to be acquired in each stage of the human life cycle	

Chapter 2 Responsibilities of Parenting
Section 2.1 Parenting and Families

 Note Taking

Directions As you read, write notes, facts, and main ideas in the Note Taking column. Write key words and short phrases in the Cues column. Then summarize the section in the Summary box.

Cues	Note Taking
• the role of parenting	**PREPARATION FOR PARENTHOOD** • Being a parent is one of the most important roles a person has in life.
• becoming a parent	**PARENTING RESPONSIBILITIES AND REWARDS** • Parents feel great joy when a new child joins the family.

Summary

Parenting is a learning process.

Chapter 2 Responsibilities of Parenting

Section 2.1 Parenting and Families

 Mathematics
Creating a Budget

> **NCTM Number and Operations** Compute fluently and make reasonable estimates.

Directions Jack and Sue have a monthly net income of $4,050. They plan to have a baby in about a year and would like to save $10,000 to pay for medical expenses. Using the budget sheet, revise their current budget to figure out how they can save $10,000 over the course of one year. Then explain your plan.

Monthly Living Expenses	Original Budget	Revised Budget
Fixed Expenses		
Rent	$1,250	
Car Payments	$530	
Insurance Payments	$200	
Emergency Fund	$50	
Savings	$300	
Household Expenses		
Food and Groceries	$750	
Utilities	$105	
Telephone	$150	
Transportation	$175	
Personal Spending		
Clothing	$250	
Gifts	$50	
Pocket Money	$100	
Recreation	$140	
Total	**$4,050**	

_____

_____

_____

Chapter 2 Responsibilities of Parenting
Section 2.1 Parenting and Families

Study Skills
Using Flash Cards

Directions Follow the directions to make flash cards to use as study aids. Use the space below to organize your information.

- Use 3- by 5-inch index cards.
- Create questions from headings, key words, end-of-section questions, end-of-chapter questions, and any questions in the text. Write your question on one side of the index card.
- On the back of the index card, write the answer to the question.
- Review the cards in random order. Look at the front of the card. Read the questions aloud. Then answer the question.
- Turn the card over to review the answer.

Front of Card

What kinds of conflicting or difficult emotions do parents sometimes feel?

Back of Card

- Fear of not being a good parent.
- Frustration at the loss of personal freedom and the addition of new responsibilities.
- Worry over money matters.
- Jealousy of the baby and the attention he or she gets from the other parent, friends, and relatives.
- Depression due to exhaustion and the physical challenges of pregnancy and birth.

Chapter 2

Chapter 2 Responsibilities of Parenting
Section 2.2 Teen Parenthood

 Note Taking

Directions As you read, write notes, facts, and main ideas in the Note
Taking column. Write key words and short phrases in the Cues column.
Then summarize the section in the Summary box.

Cues	Note Taking
• sexuality	**SEXUAL DEVELOPMENT** • Sexuality involves people's feelings about themselves and a sense of responsibility for and understanding of others' feelings.
• abstinence	**ABSTINENCE** • Choosing abstinence allows you to take responsibility for your well-being.
• STIs	**CONSEQUENCES OF SEXUAL ACTIVITY** • Saying yes to sexual pressures as a teen can cause difficulties in future relationships and loss of self-respect.
• consequences	**TEEN PARENTING OPTIONS** • Pregnant teens' options include marriage, single parent-hood, and adoption.
• fidelity	**TAKE RESPONSIBILITY** • Sexual responsibility means knowing the facts about sexuality, and basing your decisions on values.

Summary
Decisions related to sexuality cannot be made casually.

Chapter 2

Chapter 2 Responsibilities of Parenting

Section 2.2 Teen Parenthood

 Social Studies
Compare Cultural Values

NCSS IV F Individual Development and Identity Analyze the role of perceptions, attitudes, values, and beliefs in the development of personal identity.

Directions The term *family values* means different things to different people. Values may be based on such things as family tradition, religion, or culture. For example, Hispanic cultures promote the value of a close-knit family. Make a list of the five most important values you feel you learned from your family. Then ask two other friends or classmates from a different culture to list five important values they learned from their families. Note what cultural background the person's family is from. Were their values different from your own? Write a brief report summarizing your findings.

_____

_____

_____

_____

_____

_____

_____

_____

_____

_____

_____

_____

_____

_____

_____

_____

_____

_____

_____

Chapter 2 Responsibilities of Parenting

Section 2.2 Teen Parenthood

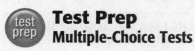 **Test Prep**
Multiple-Choice Tests

Directions Read these tips to help you take multiple-choice tests. Then fill in the circle next to the word or phrase that best answers each question.

Taking Multiple-Choice Tests
• Cover the answer choices.
• Read the question.
• Try to answer the question before looking at the answer choices.
• Read all the answer choices.
• Eliminate answer choices you know are wrong.
• Mark the answer choice you think is correct.
• Do not go back and change your answer. Your first choice is usually correct.

1. _____ stress may be consequences of sexual activity.
   ○ Social and academic   ○ Emotional and academic
   ● Emotional and social   ○ Academic and physical

2. Messages about sexual activity _____.
   ○ are directed only at mature adults   ○ seem to be everywhere
   ○ can be easily avoided   ○ do not exist

3. _____ allows you to take responsibility for your own well-being.
   ○ Becoming sexually active
   ○ Discussing sexuality with a friend
   ○ Choosing abstinence
   ○ Avoiding teens of the opposite gender

4. One role of families is to pass along society's _____.
   ○ problems   ○ concerns
   ○ illnesses   ○ values

5. Holding hands, hugging, and kissing are _____ ways of showing love.
   ○ nonsexual   ○ nonphysical
   ○ sexual   ○ unimportant

6. Chlamydia can be cured with _____.
   ○ rest   ○ abstinence
   ○ antibiotics   ○ aspirin

Chapter 2

Chapter 2 Responsibilities of Parenting

Chapter Vocabulary

 English Language Arts
Fill in the Blank

NCTE12 Use language to accomplish individual purposes.

Directions For each blank in the paragraph, write in the vocabulary term that makes the most sense in the sentence.

- sexuality
- hormone
- sexually transmitted infection (STI)
- abstinence
- paternity
- fidelity
- intimacy
- essential

During adolescence, when _____hormones_____ are causing physical changes

that lead to sexual maturity, young people must be in touch with their

_____, or beliefs and values about sexual behavior. Knowing

your values and choosing _____ as a deliberate decision shows

that you take responsibility for your own well-being. When young people avoid

sexual activity, they can rest assured that they will not contract a

_____. Teens who choose to avoid sexual activity may opt for

other forms of _____ such as spending time together enjoying

shared interests. Teens who become pregnant face many consequences such as

health risks, education challenges, financial issues, and emotional and social stress.

Many people choose to wait until they are married before engaging in sexual

activity. They want a relationship based on _____, or faithfulness

to an obligation, duty, or trust.

Chapter 2

Chapter 3 Building Strong Families

Section 3.1 Family Characteristics

 Note Taking

Directions As you read, write notes, facts, and main ideas in the Note Taking column. Write key words and short phrases in the Cues column. Then summarize the section in the Summary box.

Cues	Note Taking
• families are vital	**QUALITIES OF STRONG FAMILIES** • Families are the foundation for every human culture.
• nuclear family	**FAMILY STRUCTURE** • A nuclear family includes one or more children and two parents.
• intergenerational	**TRENDS AFFECTING FAMILIES** • All families are affected by societal trends.

Summary
Families today serve many functions.

Chapter 3

Chapter 3 Building Strong Families

Section 3.1 Family Characteristics

 English Language Arts
Persuasive Paragraph

NCTE 5 Use different writing process elements to communicate effectively.

Directions Read the Expert Advice quotation.
Then, on the lines provided, write a persuasive paragraph in which you
agree or disagree with the quotation. You should state your position
clearly and back up your opinion with as many facts as possible.

Expert Advice
"The family is the corner stone of our society. More than any other force it shapes the attitude, the hopes, the ambitions, and the values of the child." —*Lyndon Baines Johnson, former U.S. president*

_____

_____

_____

_____

_____

_____

_____

_____

_____

_____

_____

_____

_____

_____

_____

_____

_____

Chapter 3

Chapter 3 Building Strong Families

Section 3.1 Family Characteristics

 Study Skills
Study Strategies

Directions Read the study strategies. Then fill in the bubble next to the word that best completes the sentence or answers the question.

Study Strategies
• Use a monthly calendar to record assignments as soon as you learn about them. Include the assignment's due date, and schedule study times to complete the assignment on time.
• Use a different color pen for each class.
• Record upcoming test dates. Highlight these dates. Block out extra study time.

1. Strong families _____.
   - ○ are all very similar in their makeup
   - ● have a variety of characteristics
   - ○ do not have time to deal with family controversies
   - ○ rely on others to provide for them

2. Families prepare children to live in society _____.
   - ○ through family, friends, and others
   - ○ through government programs
   - ○ through example, communication, and religious training
   - ○ by paying experts to teach their children what they need to know to survive

3. _____ are beliefs held by an individual, family, community or society.
   - ○ Assumptions
   - ○ Heritages
   - ○ Values
   - ○ Laws

4. Which of the following can help handle family conflict?
   - ○ screaming and yelling
   - ○ walking away
   - ○ hitting
   - ○ being an active listener

5. Intergenerational means occurring between older and younger _____.
   - ○ age groups
   - ○ teens
   - ○ siblings
   - ○ children

Chapter 3 Building Strong Families
Section 3.2 Parenting Skills

 Note Taking

Directions As you read, write notes, facts, and main ideas in the Note Taking column. Write key words and short phrases in the Cues column. Then summarize the section in the Summary box.

Cues	Note Taking
• deprivation	**CHILDREN'S NEEDS** • Having a child does not make a person an effective parent.
• parenting style	**PARENTING STYLES** • There are three main parenting styles.
• dispute	**GUIDE CHILDREN'S BEHAVIOR** • Children need to be taught what is acceptable, what is not acceptable, and what is expected of them.

Summary
Parents use many skills to raise children.

Chapter 3

Chapter 3 Building Strong Families
Section 3.2 Parenting Skills

 Social Studies
Appropriate Punishment

> **NCSS IV I Individual Development and Identity** Examine factors that contribute to and damage one's mental health and analyze issues related to mental health and behavioral disorders in contemporary society.

Directions Read the scenario. Then choose the most appropriate punishment. Write a paragraph to explain how the child might be harmed if inappropriate punishment is used.

Five-year-old Alicia was kicking the ball in the house. She knew it was against the rules. Suddenly, the ball hit a vase, an heirloom that had been in her mother's family for over one hundred years. The vase crashed to the floor smashed to pieces. Alicia's mother heard the noise and came running from the kitchen. Seeing the vase and the ball, she immediately understood what had happened.

Which of the following do you think would be the most appropriate punishment for Alicia? Circle the letter of your choice.

a. Alicia is not allowed to play with the ball for a week.

b. Alicia's mother tells her she is the clumsiest child she has ever seen.

c. Alicia's mother screams at her.

d. Alicia is given a time-out for 15 minutes.

_____

_____

_____

_____

_____

_____

_____

_____

_____

_____

Chapter 3

Chapter 3 Building Strong Families
Section 3.2 Parenting Skills

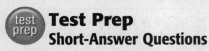 **Test Prep**
Short-Answer Questions

Directions Read the tips for answering short-answer questions, then
write short answers to the questions below.

Answering Short-Answer Questions
• Read the questions carefully. Look for key words.   • Make notes on another piece of paper about the facts and important information for your answer.   • Organize your notes.   • Write two or three short sentences.   • Include as much information as possible in your answer.

1. Why do children need to be taught what is acceptable and unacceptable and
what is expected of them?

_____

_____

_____

_____

_____

_____

_____

2. Why should parents give a warning before punishing a child?

_____

_____

_____

_____

_____

_____

_____

Chapter 3 Building Strong Families

Chapter Vocabulary

 English Language Arts
Sentence Completion

> **NCTE 12** Use language to accomplish individual purposes.

Directions Write the vocabulary term that best completes each sentence.

- deprivation
- parenting style
- guidance
- self-discipline
- conscience

- positive reinforcement
- negative reinforcement
- time-out
- dispute
- consistent

1. Children who are able to control their own behavior are exhibiting ___self-discipline___.

2. _____ encourages children to repeat a particular behavior.

3. Parents must be _____ to successfully guide children's behavior.

4. Children suffer from _____ when their parents cannot or do not meet all of their physical, emotional, social, or intellectual needs.

5. _____ strengthens desired behavior by removing an unpleasant trigger.

6. Parents who help their children learn how to behave are providing _____.

7. A misbehaving child might be given a _____ to provide time for the child to calm down and regain self-control.

8. As children mature, they use their _____ to help them decide how to behave in new situations.

9. Children must be taught effective ways to settle a _____.

10. Parents use a _____ they are comfortable with when they care for and discipline their children.

Chapter 4 Prenatal Development

Section 4.1 The Developing Baby

 Note Taking

Directions As you read, write notes, facts, and main ideas in the Note Taking column. Write key words and short phrases in the Cues column. Then summarize the section in the Summary box.

Cues	Note Taking
• ovum	**FAMILY PLANNING** • Pregnancy can result anytime a couple has sexual intercourse.
• prenatal development	**THREE STAGES OF PREGNANCY** • Prenatal development includes the germinal stage, embryonic stage, and fetal stage.

Summary

Anytime sexual intercourse occurs, pregnancy may occur.

Chapter 4 Prenatal Development

Section 4.1 The Developing Baby

English Language Arts
Stages of Development

NCTE 12 Use language to accomplish individual purposes.

Directions Create a flow chart that shows the stages of a baby's development from conception through pregnancy. Include a brief explanation for each stage. Use a rectangle for the main stages and an oval for development that occurs within a stage.

conception the process of the sperm fertilizing the ovum	→	**germinal stage** the first stage in a baby's development	→	**cell division** begins in the fallopian tube	→

Chapter 4

Chapter 4 Prenatal Development
Section 4.1 The Developing Baby

 Study Skills
Using Your Notes

Directions Read the tips for using your notes. Refer to your notes as you complete the following exercise. Write the number of the month of fetal development that is described.

Tips for Using Your Notes
• Use highlighters to color code your notes for visual stimulation. • Rewrite your notes on a different sheet of paper. Continue to rewrite your notes until you have memorized them. • Read your notes into an audio recorder, and then listen to the notes again and again until you have the information memorized.

Month-by-Month Development

_____7_____ about 10 to 12 inches long; weighs about 1 ½ to 2 pounds; has periods of activity followed by periods of rest and quiet

_____ about 3 inches long; weighs 1 ounce; can suck thumb, swallow, hiccup, and move around; facial features become clearer

_____ size of a pinhead; egg attaches to lining of uterus; critical stage for brain and spinal cord development; internal organs and circulatory system begin to form; heart begins to beat

_____ about 17 to 18 inches long; weighs about 5 to 6 pounds; movements decrease; acquires disease-fighting antibodies; descends into pelvis

_____ about 14 to 16 inches long; weighs about 2 ½ to 3 pounds; rapid weight gain; moves to head-down position

_____ about 8 to 10 inches long; weighs about 8 to 12 ounces; fetus appears wrinkled; breathing movements begin

_____ about ¼ inch long; face, eyes, ears, and limbs take shape; bones begin to form

_____ about 1 inch long; nostrils, mouth, and eyelids form; buds for baby teeth appear; fingers and toes almost complete; organs present, but immature

_____ about 6 ½ to 7 inches long; weighs 4 to 5 ounces; hair, eyelashes, and eyebrows appear; organs are maturing; becomes more active

Chapter 4 Prenatal Development

Section 4.2 Problems in Prenatal Development

 Note Taking

Directions As you read, write notes, facts, and main ideas in the Note Taking column. Write key words and short phrases in the Cues column. Then summarize the section in the Summary box.

Cues	Note Taking
• miscarriage	**LOSING A BABY** • Most babies develop normally and are born healthy.
• ultrasound tests	**BIRTH DEFECTS** • Approximately 120,000 U.S. babies each year are born with a birth defect.

Summary

Some pregnancies end in miscarriage or stillbirth.

Chapter 4

Chapter 4 Prenatal Development
Section 4.2 Problems in Prenatal Development

 Social Studies
Treatment of Birth Defects

NCSS VIII B Science, Technology, and Society Make judgments about how science and technology have transformed the physical world.

Directions Choose one of the birth defects listed below. Use the library or Internet to learn what research is being done now to improve the lives of people with that birth defect. Write down your findings. Be prepared to share your information with the rest of the class.

Birth Defects		
cerebral palsy	cleft lip and cleft palate	cystic fibrosis
Down syndrome	muscular dystrophy	phenylketonuria
sickle-cell anemia	spina bifida and hydrocephalus	Tay-Sachs disease

_____

_____

_____

_____

_____

_____

_____

_____

_____

_____

_____

_____

_____

_____

_____

_____

_____

Chapter 4

Chapter 4 Prenatal Development

Section 4.2 Problems in Prenatal Development

Test Prep
Taking True/False Tests

Directions Read the tips for taking true/false tests. Then take the true/false test below. Circle **T** if the statement is true or **F** if it is false.

Taking True/False Tests
• Answers are true only when every part of the statement is true. If part of the statement is false, the entire statement is false. Watch out for long sentences that include a series or list set off by commas or semicolons. Every part of the whole statement must be true.
• Watch out for words that are unqualified, such as *always, never, every,* or *none.* These usually indicate a *false* answer.
• Statements with words such as *usually, sometimes,* or *often* are usually true statements.
• Change sentences written in the negative to a positive by reading the sentence without the negative word. If the statement without the negative is true, then you know the answer with the negative is probably false.

Ⓣ F **1.** Factors in the environment can cause some types of birth defects.

T F **2.** Parents who lose a baby to miscarriage or stillbirth do not go through any stages of grief.

T F **3.** Muscular dystrophy can be cured by physical therapy.

T F **4.** Errors in chromosomes can cause some birth defects such as Down syndrome.

T F **5.** Inheriting the same faulty recessive gene from both parents can lead to a birth defect.

T F **6.** It is necessary to inherit the same faulty dominant gene from both parents for a birth defect to occur.

T F **7.** A pregnant woman who smokes or drinks alcohol increases her chances of having a baby with a birth defect.

T F **8.** It is all right for a pregnant woman to take over-the-counter medications as long as she tells her doctor afterwards.

T F **9.** An ultrasound can always detect birth defects in an unborn child.

T F **10.** Common prenatal tests include alpha-fetoprotein, ultrasound, amniocentesis, chorionic villi sampling, and genetic counseling.

Chapter 4

Chapter 4 Prenatal Development
Section 4.3 Avoiding Dangers to the Baby

 Note Taking

Directions As you read, write notes, facts, and main ideas in the Note Taking column. Write key words and short phrases in the Cues column. Then summarize the section in the Summary box.

Cues	Note Taking
	EFFECTS OF ALCOHOL AND OTHER DRUGS ON PREGNANCY
• fetal alcohol syndrome (FAS)	• Everything a pregnant woman consumes goes directly to her child through the placenta.
	ENVIRONMENTAL HAZARDS
• environmental hazards are all around us	• Radiation from X-rays and other sources can cause birth defects in unborn babies.
	DISEASES AND INFECTIONS
• Toxoplasmosis	• An infection in a pregnant woman can pose a risk for the unborn baby.

Summary
Everything a pregnant woman eats, drinks, and breathes affects her developing fetus.

Chapter 4

Chapter 4 Prenatal Development
Section 4.3 Avoiding Dangers to the Baby

 Science
Effects of Drugs on Pregnancy

NSES F Understanding of personal and community health; natural and human-induced hazards.

Directions Fill in the graphic organizer with alcohol and other drugs and the potential hazards they can cause an unborn baby.

Alcohol
Alcohol can cause fetal alcohol syndrome, which can lead to delayed physical growth; heart, liver, or kidney defects; hyperactivity; facial deformity; and mental retardation.

Effects
of Drugs
on Pregnancy

Chapter 4

Chapter 4 Prenatal Development
Chapter Vocabulary

 English Language Arts
Writing Paragraphs

NCTE 12 Use language to accomplish individual purposes.

Directions Write one or more paragraphs that use at least 10 of the vocabulary terms. Sentences should demonstrate your understanding of the terms. Use the following guidelines for writing your paragraphs.

- Each paragraph focuses on one main idea.
- All the sentences in each paragraph support the main idea.
- You have used transition words to link ideas.

• amniocentesis	• fetus	• stillbirth
• amniotic fluid	• gene	• surrogate
• chromosome	• genome	• toxoplasmosis
• conception	• infertility	• ultrasound
• DNA	• miscarriage	• umbilical cord
• embryo	• ovum	• uterus
• fallopian tube	• placenta	• zygote
• fetal alcohol effects	• prenatal development	
• fetal alcohol syndrome (FAS)	• SIDS	
	• sperm	

_____

_____

_____

_____

_____

_____

_____

_____

_____

_____

_____

_____

_____

Chapter 4

Chapter 5 Preparing for Birth

Section 5.1 A Healthy Pregnancy

 Note Taking

Directions As you read, write notes, facts, and main ideas in the Note Taking column. Write key words and short phrases in the Cues column. Then summarize the section in the Summary box.

Cues	Note Taking
• signs of pregnancy	**HEALTH DURING PREGNANCY** • A pregnant woman's responsibilities grow along with her fetus.
• five food groups	**NUTRITION DURING PREGNANCY** • Good nutrition is the single most important requirement during pregnancy.

Summary
A woman should see a doctor as soon as she believes she is pregnant.

Chapter 5

Chapter 5 Preparing for Birth

Section 5.1 A Healthy Pregnancy

Science
Pregnancy Dos and Don'ts

Directions Read the paragraphs about things a woman should and should not do during pregnancy. Fill in the blanks with words from the word list that make the most sense.

> **NSES C** Develop understanding of the cell; molecular basis of heredity; matter, energy, and organization in living systems.

Word List		
• childbirth	• maintain	• pregnancy
• complaint	• medical	• responsibility
• exercising	• monitor	• rest
• healthful	• objects	• suffer
• hygiene	• obstetrician	• weight

Pregnancy Dos and Don'ts

Women who are pregnant must be careful to take care of not only themselves, but also their unborn baby. Because of this ___responsibility___, there are some things pregnant women should do, and some things they should not do.

Pregnant women should have regular _____ checkups with an _____, or doctor who specializes in _____ and _____. He or she can be especially helpful to women who experience discomfort during pregnancy. Lower back pain is a common _____ among pregnant women. Pregnant women who _____ from lower back pain should not wear high-heeled shoes and should avoid lifting heavy _____.

Pregnant women should _____ themselves by stepping on a scale regularly. Gaining too little _____ can increase the risk of fetal death or premature birth. Eating a _____ diet can help a pregnant woman _____ the proper weight. Other routines that will help a pregnant woman stay healthy include getting plenty of _____, _____, and practicing good _____.

Chapter 5 Preparing for Birth

Section 5.1 A Healthy Pregnancy

 Study Skills
Reading Charts

Directions A chart is a visual representation that allows several different things to be compared. Use the chart to answer the questions about the recommended nutrition intake of a 27-year-old pregnant woman.

MyPyramid for Moms
Recommended Daily Intake

	1st Trimester	2nd Trimester	3rd Trimester
Grains	7 ounces	9 ounces	9 ounces
Vegetables	3 cups	3 ½ cups	3 ½ cups
Fruits	2 cups	2 cups	2 cups
Milk	3 cups	3 cups	3 cups
Meat and Beans	6 ounces	6 ½ ounces	6 ½ ounces

Source: www.MyPyramid.gov

1. How much milk should this pregnant woman consume each day during the third trimester of her pregnancy?

   _____

2. How much more meat and beans should this woman consume daily during the second trimester than she consumed during the first trimester?

   _____

3. How much grain should this woman consume each day during her first trimester?

   _____

4. What is the total amount of grains, vegetables, fruits, milk, and meat and beans this woman should eat daily during her first trimester?

   _____

5. How much meat and beans should this woman consume during her third trimester?

   _____

6. For which foods does the amount stay the same for each trimester?

   _____

Chapter 5

Chapter 5 Preparing for Birth

Section 5.2 Preparing for the Baby's Arrival

 Note Taking

Directions As you read, write notes, facts, and main ideas in the Note Taking column. Write key words and short phrases in the Cues column. Then summarize the section in the Summary box.

Cues	Note Taking
• basic supplies	**PREPARING FOR PARENTHOOD** • Pregnancy is a time for expectant parents to prepare for meeting their baby's physical, emotional, and intellectual needs.
• fixed expense	**MAKING A BUDGET** • Prenatal care is an important expense that can be quite costly.

Summary
Parents-to-be should prepare for the birth of the child.

Chapter 5

Chapter 5 Preparing for Birth

Section 5.2 Preparing for the Baby's Arrival

 Mathematics
Planning Baby's Room

NCTM Measurement Understand measurable attributes of objects and the units, systems, and processes of measurement.

Directions Imagine that you need to set up a baby's room with all of the necessary furniture. First, list the pieces of furniture you will need in the room. Next, look through catalogs to find the dimensions of the pieces of furniture. Then use the grid below to arrange the furniture in the baby's room. Each square represents one square foot of floor space.

Furniture Needed
Crib _____

_____

_____

Dimensions
5 feet by 3 feet _____

_____

_____

Door

Window

Closet

Chapter 5

Chapter 5 Preparing for Birth

Section 5.2 Preparing for the Baby's Arrival

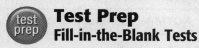 **Test Prep**
Fill-in-the-Blank Tests

Directions Read the tips for taking fill-in-the-blank tests. Then use words from the word list to fill in the blanks to complete the sentences.

Fill-in-the-Blank Tests
• Carefully read all the words before answering each statement. Think about what each word means.
• Carefully read each statement.
• Fill in the statements you are sure of with the best word choice. Some words may be close, so make sure you choose the best word.
• Cross off the words as you use them to avoid using them again.
• Once you have eliminated the words you are sure of, go back over the words you are less sure of and reread each statement. Fill in the blank with the best choice.
• Check the word list to make sure you have used all the words.
• Reread all the statements to make sure each one has an answer that makes sense.

Word List

- age
- bath
- brother
- unattended
- change
- clothes
- elevated
- emotional
- intellectual
- physical
- safety
- sister
- travel

1. New parents must decide how to meet their baby's ___physical___, ___emotional___, and ___intellectual___ needs.

2. How children react to a new _____ or _____ depends on how well prepared they were before the baby's arrival, how they react to _____, and their _____.

3. Babies need _____, bedding, _____ supplies, and _____ equipment.

4. Crib _____ should be a high priority.

5. A baby should never be left _____ on any _____ surface such as a changing table or bed, even if restraint straps are used.

Chapter 5 Preparing for Birth
Section 5.3 Childbirth Options

 Note Taking

Directions As you read, write notes, facts, and main ideas in the Note Taking column. Write key words and short phrases in the Cues column. Then summarize the section in the Summary box.

Cues	Note Taking
• prepared childbirth	**PREPARED CHILDBIRTH** • Many expectant parents attend childbirth classes to help them prepare for labor and delivery.
• midwife	**DELIVERY OPTIONS** • There are many options for where a baby will be born and the type of health care professional who will attend the birth.

Summary
Prepared childbirth helps expectant parents get ready for labor and delivery.

Chapter 5

Chapter 5 Preparing for Birth
Section 5.3 Childbirth Options

 English Language Arts
Comparing Delivery Options

NCTE 5 Use different writing process elements to communicate effectively.

Directions Write two paragraphs in which you compare and contrast delivery options. In the first paragraph, you should discuss health care professionals. In the second paragraph, you should discuss different places to give birth.

Delivery Options

Obstetricians specialize in the care of mothers and babies both before and right after birth, and are qualified to handle any emergencies or problems that might occur.

_____
_____
_____
_____
_____
_____
_____
_____
_____
_____
_____
_____
_____
_____
_____
_____
_____
_____
_____

Chapter 5 Preparing for Birth

Chapter Vocabulary

 English Language Arts
Matching Definitions

NCTE 12 Use language
to accomplish individual
purposes.

Directions Choose the vocabulary term from the list
that best matches each definition. Write the word in the right column of
the table. Note: You will not use all of the terms.

Content Vocabulary		Academic Vocabulary
• alternative birth center • maternity leave		• alleviate
• anemia • midwife		• complication
• delivery • obstetrician		• compressed
• fixed expense • osteoporosis		• reimbursement
• flexible expense • paternity leave		• robust
• formula • pediatrician		• slat
• gestational diabetes • preeclampsia		
• labor • prepared childbirth		
• lactase • Rh factor		
• lactose intolerance		

Definition	Word
a condition that results from not having enough red blood cells	anemia
an expense that can be changed, such as food costs, clothes, and entertainment	
a condition characterized by high blood pressure and the presence of protein in the mother's urine	
thriving	
a health care professional trained to assist women in childbirth	
a condition in which milk products cause symptoms such as abdominal pain and gas	
a payment that generally cannot be changed	
a facility that provides a more homelike environment for labor and delivery	
a form of diabetes that occurs only during pregnancy	
a condition in which bones are fragile and break easily	

Chapter 5

Name _____ Date _____ Class _____

Chapter 6 The Baby's Arrival
Section 6.1 Labor and Birth

 Note Taking

Directions As you read, write notes, facts, and main ideas in the Note Taking column. Write key words and short phrases in the Cues column. Then summarize the section in the Summary box.

Cues	Note Taking
• cervix	**THE PROGRESSION OF LABOR** • Giving birth is a powerful physical and emotional experience.
• cesarean births	**CESAREAN BIRTH** • Cesarean birth is delivery of a baby through a surgical incision.
• incubator	**PREMATURE BIRTH** • Five to six percent of all babies are born prematurely.

Summary

There are three main stages of labor: contractions open the cervix, the baby is born, and the placenta is expelled.

Chapter 6 The Baby's Arrival
Section 6.1 Labor and Birth

Social Studies
International Birthing Practices

Directions Choose a country other than the United States. Use the library or Internet to research birthing practices used in that country. Write a one-page report in which you explain the process in as much detail as possible. Be sure to check your report and correct any grammar or spelling errors.

_____

_____

_____

_____

_____

_____

_____

_____

_____

_____

_____

_____

_____

Chapter 6 The Baby's Arrival
Section 6.1 Labor and Birth

 Study Skills
Proofreading

Directions Read the tips for proofreading. Then use them to proofread the paragraph.

Proofreading
• Use a ruler to help you focus on one line at a time. • Read the text aloud. • Look for grammar and punctuation errors, misspellings, and clarity. • Circle any mistakes you find. • Write corrections in the margin next to the mistake.

Childbirth Education Classes

Many expectent parents attend childbirth education classes to help them prepare for labor. Classes may be offered by hospitals, health care providers, or private teachers.

Childbirth education classes offered by hospitals may also included a tour of the facility. Parents-to-be are shown where to go when they arrive and where they will be during labor and delivery, and after delivery. classes might also review specific rules of the hospital regarding visitors, support persons, and electronics. For example, some hospitals will not allow camras in the delivery room. Most hospitals have specified areas where cell phones can be used.

Classes will also help parents make a plan for the labor and delivery. This are called a birth plan. This tells the medical staff what the couple would like to have happen during the childbirth process, including the possible use of Pain medication.

Chapter 6 The Baby's Arrival

Section 6.2 The Newborn

 Note Taking

Directions As you read, write notes, facts, and main ideas in the Note Taking column. Write key words and short phrases in the Cues column. Then summarize the section in the Summary box.

Cues	Note Taking
• fontanel	**THE BABY ARRIVES** • A newborn goes through physical changes needed for its survival outside the mother.
• Apgar scale	**EXAMINING THE NEWBORN** • Newborns' physical condition is evaluated using the Apgar scale.

Summary

At birth, the newborn baby changes physically in several ways.

Chapter 6

Chapter 6 The Baby's Arrival
Section 6.2 The Newborn

 Mathematics
Calculate Baby's Weight Change

> **NCTM Problem Solving** Solve problems that arise in mathematics and in other contexts.

Directions Use the information provided in the chart to answer the questions. Show the problem you solved to calculate your answer. Remember: 1 pound = 16 ounces.

Babies' Weights				
	Birth	**3 months**	**6 months**	**9 months**
Baby A	7 lbs. 8 oz.	13 lbs.	17 lbs. 8 oz.	20 lbs. 8 oz.
Baby B	7 lbs. 4 oz.	12 lbs. 6 oz.	15 lbs. 8 oz.	21 lbs.
Baby C	6 lbs. 12 oz.	12 lbs.	14 lbs. 14 oz.	20 lbs.

1. How much weight did Baby A gain from birth to 9 months?

_____

2. If you put all three 9-month-old babies on the scale at the same time, how much would they weigh?

_____

3. How much more did Baby A weigh at birth than Baby B?

_____

4. How much weight did Baby C gain from birth to 6 months?

_____

5. How much less did Baby A weigh at 3 months than at 9 months?

_____

6. What is the total of all three babies' weights at 3 months?

_____

7. What is the difference in weights of Babies A and B at 6 months?

_____

8. Which baby weighed the most at 9 months of age? Which weighed the least?

_____

Chapter 6 The Baby's Arrival
Section 6.2 The Newborn

 **Test Prep**
Essay Tests

Directions Read the information on taking essay tests. Then use it to write an essay to answer the question.

Essay Tests
• Essay questions do not require a lot of writing. Instead, answer the specific question by using as few words as possible. Your grade will be determined by how well you answer the questions, not how long your answer is. • Give specific information and facts, cite details, and provide examples to support your answer. • In the first paragraph, answer the question directly and state the main points of the essay. You should have two or three points. • In the next two paragraphs, explain your main points with supporting details. • In the last paragraph, summarize the main points. • Reread what you have written. Check for spelling, punctuation, and clarity.

1. What are the exams and procedures given to a newborn in the first few days?

    When babies are born, their condition is usually evaluated using the Apgar scale.

    _____

    _____

    _____

    _____

    _____

    _____

    _____

    _____

    _____

    _____

    _____

    _____

    _____

    _____

Chapter 6 The Baby's Arrival

Section 6.3 The Postnatal Period

 Note Taking

Directions As you read, write notes, facts, and main ideas in the Note Taking column. Write key words and short phrases in the Cues column. Then summarize the section in the Summary box.

Cues	Note Taking
• neonatal period	**AFTER THE BIRTH** • The neonatal period involves major adjustments for mother and baby.
• postnatal period	**MOTHER'S POSTNATAL CARE** • A new mother has special needs during the postnatal period.

Summary
Bonding after birth strengthens the emotional connection between parents and their child.

Chapter 6 The Baby's Arrival

Section 6.3 The Postnatal Period

English Language Arts
Create a Brochure

NCTE 4 Use written language to communicate effectively.

Directions Use information from the text to create a brochure that explains the mother's experience following the birth of the baby. Be sure to explain what the mother will be feeling physically, mentally, and emotionally. Also include what the mother will be watching the baby go through immediately after birth. Be creative and include illustrations in your brochure. Check your brochure and correct any spelling or grammar errors. Use the space below to plan your brochure.

1 Left Inside Panel	2 Middle Inside Panel	3 Right Inside Panel

4 Inside Flap	5 Back Panel	6 Front Cover

Chapter 6 The Baby's Arrival

Chapter Vocabulary

English Language Arts
Writing Sentences

NCTE 12 Use language to accomplish individual purposes.

Directions Choose 8 of the vocabulary terms. Find the terms in the text and read the sentences from the text where they are used. Then rewrite the sentences in your own words to demonstrate your understanding of the terms.

Content Vocabulary		Academic Vocabulary
• Apgar scale	• incubator	• anesthesia
• bilirubin	• jaundice	• fuse
• bonding	• lactation consultant	• induce
• cervix	• lanugo	• major
• cesarean birth	• neonatal period	• secure
• colostrum	• postnatal period	• stable
• contraction	• postpartum depression	
• cord blood	• rooming-in	
• dilate	• stem cells	
• fetal monitoring	• vernix	
• fontanel		

1. _____

2. _____

3. _____

4. _____

5. _____

6. _____

7. _____

8. _____

Chapter 7 Physical Development of Infants
Section 7.1 Infant Growth and Development

 Note Taking

Directions As you read, write notes, facts, and main ideas in the Note Taking column. Write key words and short phrases in the Cues column. Then summarize the section in the Summary box.

Cues	Note Taking
• developmental mile-stones	**INFLUENCES ON GROWTH AND DEVELOPMENT** • Babies experience a tremendous amount of growth and development in their first year.
• growth chart	**GROWTH AND DEVELOPMENT DURING THE FIRST YEAR** • During the first year, babies typically triple their birth weight.

Summary
Heredity, nutrition, health, and environment all play a role in a baby's growth and development.

Chapter 7

Chapter 7 Physical Development of Infants

Section 7.1 Infant Growth and Development

Science
Influences on a Child's Growth and Development

> **NSES F** Students should develop understanding of personal and community health; environmental quality.

Directions Choose one of the topics. Use the Internet or library to research the topic to learn more about how it affects a baby's growth and development. Use the information you find to write a one-page report. Reports should include informative paragraphs with a topic sentence and supportive details.

Topics

- heredity
- nutrition
- health
- environment

_____

_____

_____

_____

_____

_____

_____

_____

_____

_____

_____

_____

_____

_____

_____

_____

_____

Chapter 7 Physical Development of Infants
Section 7.1 Infant Growth and Development

 Study Skills
Mapping Main Points

Directions Read Section 1, Infant Growth and Development. As you read the text, identify several main points. Write the main points in the left column. In the right column, write details or examples that support the main points.

Main Points Map	
Main Points	**Supporting Details**
Influences on Growth and Development	• Heredity • Nutrition • Health • Environment

Chapter 7 Physical Development of Infants
Section 7.2 Caring for an Infant

 Note Taking

Directions As you read, write notes, facts, and main ideas in the Note Taking column. Write key words and short phrases in the Cues column. Then, summarize the section in the Summary box.

Cues	Note Taking
• careful handling	**HANDLING A BABY** • Babies need to be handled to be changed, fed, bathed, dressed, cuddled, and hugged.
• breast milk	**FEEDING AN INFANT** • Mealtimes provide nutrients babies need for growth and development.
• overdressed	**DRESSING A BABY** • Babies are sensitive to overheating.

Summary
Babies must be handled carefully and must never be shaken.

Chapter 7 Physical Development of Infants
Section 7.2 Caring for an Infant

English Language Arts
How to Hold a Baby

> **NCTE 8** Use information resources to gather information and create and communicate knowledge.

Directions Create a presentation for your class about how to pick up and hold a baby. Your presentation should include illustrations and text that thoroughly explain safe and correct ways to pick up and hold a baby. You should also write a script to read for the presentation.

As you plan and write your presentation, determine whether your purpose is to inform, persuade, entertain, or describe. Consider the aspects of a topic that would be suitable for your audience.

Use the space below to plan your presentation. Include ideas for illustrations, topics for text, and notes for your speech.

_____

_____

_____

_____

_____

_____

_____

_____

_____

_____

_____

_____

_____

_____

_____

_____

Chapter 7

Chapter 7 Physical Development of Infants

Section 7.2 Caring for an Infant

test prep

Test Prep
Reducing Test-Taking Anxiety

Directions Use these tips to help you reduce anxiety when taking tests.
Then circle **T** or **F** to indicate whether each statement is true or false.

Reducing Anxiety When Taking Tests
• Know the material by studying in advance.
• Maintain a positive, confident attitude.
• Get a good night's rest.
• Stay relaxed.
• Read the test directions carefully. Ask the teacher to explain any directions you do not understand.
• Pace yourself and leave time to answer all the questions.
• Build confidence by answering the simple questions first.
• Stay focused on your own test.
• Skip any questions you do not know until you have answered the questions you do know. Be sure to go back and answer any questions you skipped.

1. A newborn's muscles are not strong enough to support its head. (T)/ F

2. Pillows and stuffed toys in the crib pose no danger for newborn babies. T / F

3. Babies may cry because of a wet diaper, feeling cold or hungry, or feeling pain or sick. T / F

4. Rocking, talking, and singing can often comfort a crying baby. T / F

5. Babies should never be shaken. T / F

6. Babies under one year old should be fed cow's milk. T / F

7. A baby's stomach is large enough to allow him to sleep through the night when the baby weighs 10 pounds. T / F

8. Antibodies are substances produced by the body to fight off germs. T / F

9. Applesauce is the first solid food given to babies. T / F

10. A baby's age is the most reliable guide to a baby's clothing size. T / F

Chapter 7 Physical Development of Infants
Section 7.3 Infant Health and Wellness

 Note Taking

Directions As you read, write notes, facts, and main ideas in the Note Taking column. Write key words and short phrases in the Cues column. Then summarize the section in the Summary box.

Cues	Note Taking
• bathing a baby	**KEEPING BABY CLEAN** • Keeping a baby clean helps maintain the baby's overall wellness.
• teething	**HEALTH CARE** • Teething begins at about six months of age.

Summary
Babies should be bathed regularly.

Chapter 7

Chapter 7 Physical Development of Infants
Section 7.3 Infant Health and Wellness

 Mathematics
Finding the Mean, Median, and Mode

> **NCTM Data Analysis and Probability** Select and use appropriate statistical methods to analyze data.

Directions Read the directions for finding the mean, median, and mode for a set of numbers. Then use the information to find the mean, median, and mode for the sets of numbers provided.

To find the mean: Add the numbers, and divide by the number of items you added.
Example: Find the mean for 12, 13, 14, and 15.
First, add the numbers: 12 + 13 + 14 + 15 = 54.
Now divide by the number of items (4): 54 ÷ 4 = 13.5.
The mean is 13.5.

To find the median: Arrange the numbers in order from lowest to highest. Then find the number that is the midpoint.
Example: Find the median for 12, 15, 11, 17, and 9.
First, put the numbers in order from lowest to highest: 9, 11, 12, 15, and 17.
Now find the middle number: 12.
The median is 12.

To find the mode: Arrange the numbers in order from lowest to highest. Then find the number that occurs most frequently.
Example: Find the mode for 12, 13, 11, 15, 9, 8, 12, 15, and 12.
Arrange the numbers in order from lowest to highest: 8, 9, 11, 12, 12, 12, 13, 15, 15.
Now find the number that occurs most frequently: 12.
The mode is 12.

1. Find the mean for the weights of these babies: 8 lbs., 9 lbs., 6.5 lbs., 7 lbs.

_____

_____

2. Find the median for these babies' heights: 22 in., 23 in., 22.5 in., 23.5 in., 21 in.

_____

_____

3. Find the mode for the infant weights: 15 lbs., 14 lbs., 15 lbs., 13.5 lbs., 13.5 lbs., 14 lbs., 13.5 lbs.

_____

_____

Chapter 7 Physical Development of Infants
Chapter Vocabulary

 English Language Arts
Multiple Choice

> NCTE 12 Use language to
> accomplish individual purposes.

Directions Circle the letter for the word or phrase that best completes
each sentence.

1. A stimulating environment provides a baby with:
   a. a comfortable, safe bed.
   b. a variety of new foods to eat.
   c. a variety of things to see, taste, hear, smell, and touch.
   d. lots of toys to play with.

2. Proportion:
   a. is the same as depth perception.
   b. is the ability to perceive objects that are three-dimensional.
   c. impacts children's interaction with the world.
   d. has to do with the size relationship between different parts of the body.

3. Movements that involve muscles such as those in the fingers are called:
   a. gross motor skills.   c. large motor skills.
   b. fine motor skills.   d. little motor skills.

4. Shaken baby syndrome:
   a. can cause blindness.
   b. can lead to mental retardation.   c. can break bones.
                                              d. can do all of the above.

5. Substances in the body that fight off germs are called:
   a. antibodies.   c. reflexes.
   b. malnutrition.   d. teething.

6. When a baby is weaned:
   a. he is ready to drink from a cup rather than a bottle or breast.
   b. she no longer needs nutrients for growth and development.
   c. he eats only solid foods.
   d. she is allergic to milk.

7. Cradle cap:
   a. is caused by the baby bumping its head in the cradle.
   b. becomes worse if washed with mild shampoo.
   c. is best treated with lots of baby oil.
   d. is a skin condition known for yellowish, crusty patches on the scalp.

Chapter 8 Emotional and Social Development of Infants

Section 8.1 Understanding Emotional Development of Infants

Note Taking

Directions As you read, write notes, facts, and main ideas in the Note Taking column. Write key words and short phrases in the Cues column. Then summarize the section in the Summary box.

Cues	Note Taking
• emotional development	**EMOTIONS AND EMOTIONAL DEVELOPMENT** • Babies learn emotions through interaction with caregivers.
• attachment	**ATTACHMENT AND EMOTIONAL DEVELOPMENT** • Attachments are essential to the healthy emotional development of an infant.
• temperament	**UNDERSTANDING TEMPERAMENT** • Understanding a baby's temperament allows the caregiver to know what care is needed.
• babies sense others' emotions	**EMOTIONAL CLIMATE OF THE HOME** • Babies are influenced by adults' emotions, voice, gestures, and facial expressions.

Summary
Emotional development is the process of learning to recognize and express feelings.

Chapter 8 Emotional and Social Development of Infants

Section 8.1 Understanding Emotional Development of Infants

Social Studies
Influencing Emotional Development

> **NCSS IV C Individual Development and Identity** Describe the ways family, religion, and gender, contribute to the development of a sense of self.

Directions Write a paragraph in which you summarize the ways a child's emotional development is influenced by the family. Focus on how the family helps contribute to the child's development of a sense of self. Be sure the paragraph focuses on one main idea, all the sentences in the paragraph support the main idea, and you have used transition words to link ideas. Check your paragraph for spelling and grammar errors.

_____

_____

_____

_____

_____

_____

_____

_____

_____

_____

Chapter 8

Chapter 8 Emotional and Social Development of Infants

Section 8.1 Understanding Emotional Development of Infants

 Study Skills
Improving Reading Skills

Directions Read the tips for improving reading skills. Then read the passage and answer the questions.

Improving Reading Skills

- Turn off the radio, television, and other distractions.
- Clear your mind of outside influences.
- Read the material more than one time.
- Take notes as you read.
- Read aloud any passages that you have trouble remembering or understanding.

Babies and Colic

One research study found that giving babies a small amount of herbal tea containing chamomile, an herb that helps relax intestinal spasms, may help relieve colic. Other research indicates that symptoms of colic may be related to mild disturbances of the spinal joints. In one study, a series of gentle fingertip spinal massage techniques led to a significant reduction in colic symptoms.

Another research study indicates that the degree of tension in a baby's household may contribute to colic. The study found that the higher the emotional turmoil and tension in the household, the greater is the likelihood of colic. Maternal depression or turmoil during pregnancy may also increase the risk of colic.

1. Why were babies given a small amount of herbal tea?

   _____

2. What is chamomile?

   _____

3. According to one study, how does the degree of tension in a baby's household contribute to colic?

   _____

4. In addition to emotional turmoil and tension in the household, what may also increase a baby's risk of colic?

   _____

Chapter 8

Chapter 8 Emotional and Social Development of Infants

Section 8.2 Understanding Social Development of Infants

 Note Taking

Directions As you read, write notes, facts, and main ideas in the Note Taking column. Write key words and short phrases in the Cues column. Then summarize the section in the Summary box.

Cues	Note Taking
• social development	**SOCIAL DEVELOPMENT AND LEARNING** • Social development is a process of learning to interact and express oneself with others.
• baby's job	**SOCIAL DEVELOPMENT THROUGH PLAY** • Babies learn about the world around them through play.

Summary

Babies learn how to behave by watching and interacting with others.

Chapter 8

Chapter 8 Emotional and Social Development of Infants

Section 8.2 Understanding Social Development
of Infants

English Language Arts
Promoting Baby's Social Development

NCTE 12 Use language to accomplish individual purposes.

Directions There are many actions parents and caregivers can take to help promote a baby's social development. Write a list of actions that could be taken to promote social development in a baby. Write freely to include all of the realistic ideas that come to mind. Don't worry about an introduction or conclusion. Correct any grammar or spelling errors when you finish.

_____

_____

_____

_____

_____

_____

_____

_____

_____

_____

_____

_____

_____

_____

_____

_____

_____

_____

_____

Chapter 8 Emotional and Social Development of Infants
Section 8.2 Understanding Social Development of Infants

 Test Prep
Test-Taking Strategies

Directions Read the test-taking strategies. Then answer the questions.

Test-Taking Strategies
• Skip questions you are stuck on, and come back to them later. You might recall an answer while working on another part of the test.   • If you are unsure of the full answer to a question, answer with the part that you know. You might get partial credit.   • Write legibly. If your teacher can't read your answer, you will not get credit even if the answer is correct.

1. What behaviors are babies apt to repeat?
Babies are apt to repeat behaviors that are rewarded with love, laughter, hugs,
and praise.

2. When do babies typically begin to smile?
_____
_____

3. Why is it important to provide consistent responses to a baby's behaviors?
_____
_____

4. Describe safe toys for infants.
_____
_____

5. How does play affect a baby's social development?
_____
_____

6. What is stranger anxiety? When does it usually develop?
_____
_____

Chapter 8

Chapter 8 Emotional and Social Development of Infants
Chapter Vocabulary

English Language Arts
Matching Definitions

NCTE 12 Use language to accomplish individual purposes.

Directions Choose the content vocabulary or academic vocabulary term from the list that best matches the definition. Write the word in the right column of the table. Not all of the words will be used.

Content Vocabulary		Academic Vocabulary
• attachment	• model	• crucial
• cause and effect	• play environment	• hinder
• colic	• reflux	• motivate
• emotion	• social development	• potential
• emotional development	• stranger anxiety	
• failure to thrive	• temperament	

Definition	Word
fear of unfamiliar people, usually expressed by crying	stranger anxiety
delay or obstruct	
process of learning to recognize and express feelings and to establish a personal identity	
inspire	
teach a behavior by example	
baby's bond to his or her primary caregiver	
process of learning how to interact and express oneself with others	
critical	
condition in which partially digested food rises in the throat	
one person's unique emotional makeup	
condition in which babies do not grow and develop properly	
possible	
relationship between events in which one event is caused by another event	
uncontrollable crying by an otherwise healthy baby	
a feeling response to the world around us	

Chapter 8

Chapter 9 Intellectual Development of Infants

Section 9.1 Early Brain Development

 Note Taking

Directions As you read, write notes, facts, and main ideas in the Note Taking column. Write key words and short phrases in the Cues column. Then summarize the section in the Summary box.

Cues	Note Taking
• neuron	**THE STRUCTURE OF THE BRAIN** • Brain development happens faster in the first year than in any other time of life.
• how the brain develops	**DEVELOPING THE BRAIN** • More dendrites indicate increased learning.

Summary
Babies learn through stimulation of their senses.

Chapter 9

Chapter 9 Intellectual Development of Infants
Section 9.1 Early Brain Development

Science
Process of Development

NSES 1 Develop an understanding of science unifying concepts and processes: systems, order, and organization.

Directions Use the phrases to fill in the flowchart describing the sequence of the process within a child's brain during development. Cross out each phrase as you use it. The first one is done for you.

- Neurons grow more dendrites.
- More connections give the brain flexibility.
- Neurons create links called neural pathways.
- Neurons are connected by axons and dendrites.
- More neural pathways are created.
- More links develop between neurons.

Neurons are connected by axons and dendrites.

⬇

⬇

⬇

⬇

⬇

Chapter 9 Intellectual Development of Infants
Section 9.1 Early Brain Development

 Study Skills
Review Key Concepts

Directions In the left column, write the titles that match the summaries provided. Choose from the titles in the list. The first one is completed for you.

- Brain Structure
- How to Stimulate Brain Development in Infants
- Neural Pathways
- What Is a Dendrite?
- Learning Through Senses
- How the Brain Becomes Organized
- Parts of the Brain
- How to Speed the Brain's Work
- What Does an Axon Do?
- How Neurons Work
- What Is a Synapse?
- How Brain Power Increases

Title	Summary
Brain Structure	Neurons in a baby's brain develop neural pathways.
	Between dendrites is a tiny gap where messages are transmitted from one neuron to another.
	As connections between dendrites and axons grow stronger, a group of neurons link together forming a system of nerve cells that control a certain action.
	The more dendrites that grow and the more links that develop, the more neural pathways are created.
	The cerebrum, thalamus, cerebellum, spinal cord, pituitary gland, and brain stem work together to control body functions.
	Connections between neurons transmit instructions from the cell body to another neuron.
	Dendrites receive information from other neurons and pass information to the nerve cell; the nerve cell sends messages through axons; neurotransmitters cross the gap to the dendrite of another nerve cell.
	Links form between neurons that "wire" the brain so that it can control different body functions and thinking processes.
	Branchlike features at the end of each axon receive the messages from other neurons.
	Newborns learn about the world through what they see, hear, taste, and touch.
	Keep it simple and natural; match experience to ability level; provide practice; involve the baby; provide variety.
	Provide the child with a stimulating environment and opportunities to see, hear, smell, and touch new things.

Chapter 9

Chapter 9 Intellectual Development of Infants
Section 9.2 Intellectual Development During the First Year

 Note Taking

Directions As you read, write notes, facts, and main ideas in the Note
Taking column. Write key words and short phrases in the Cues column.
Then summarize the section in the Summary box

Cues	Note Taking
• perception	**EARLY LEARNING ABILITIES** • Newborns hear, see, taste, smell, and feel.
• Jean Piaget	**PERIODS OF LEARNING** • Psychologist Jean Piaget had a great influence on what is known about how children learn.

Summary
Babies learn by using all their senses.

Chapter 9 Intellectual Development of Infants

Section 9.2 Intellectual Development During the First Year

Social Studies
Time Line of Intellectual Growth

NCSS IV D Individual Development and Identity Apply concepts, methods, and theories about the study of human growth and development.

Directions Use the six stages of the sensorimotor period to fill in the time line with characteristics of intellectual growth a baby shows in his or her first two years.

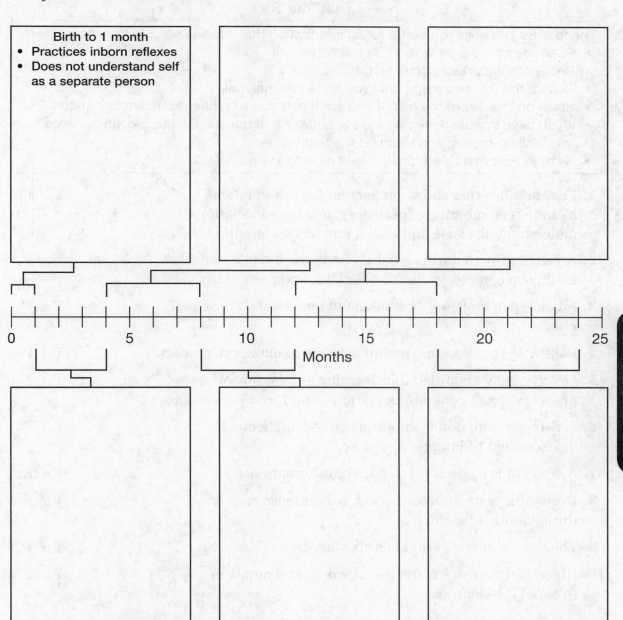

Birth to 1 month
• Practices inborn reflexes
• Does not understand self as a separate person

Months

0   5   10   15   20   25

Chapter 9

Chapter 9 Intellectual Development of Infants
Section 9.2 Intellectual Development During the First Year

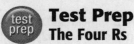 **Test Prep**
The Four Rs

Directions Read the tips for using the four Rs—read, recite, repeat, relax—to learn information that you will need to know on a test. Then take the sample true or false test shown. Circle **T** for true or **F** for false.

The Four Rs
The four Rs can help you better retain information that you will need to know on a test: • Read the material on which you will be tested. • Recite the important points aloud. • Repeat the first two steps until you know the material. • Relax on the day of the test. If you are tense, it will be hard to remember material. • If you have trouble remembering the answer to a question, relax, close your eyes, take a deep breath, and visualize the text you read. • Next, in your mind, listen to yourself reciting the material.

1. Four abilities that show intellectual growth in infants include remembering experiences, making associations, understanding cause and effect, and paying attention. **T / F**

2. Areas of growth during a baby's first year include size, intelligence, motor skills, social skills, and personality. **T / F**

3. Infants under age one are unable to understand cause and effect. **T / F**

4. Babies as young as one month are able to make eye contact. **T / F**

5. Lev Vygotsky identified four learning stages: sensorimotor, preoperational, concrete operations, and formal operations. **T / F**

6. Sensory stimulation is important to the intellectual development of infants. **T / F**

7. A concept is a specific category of information. **T / F**

8. During the sensorimotor period, babies learn mainly through direct teaching. **T / F**

9. The sensorimotor period has six stages. **T / F**

10. Object permanence is the use of words and numbers to stand for ideas. **T / F**

Chapter 9 Intellectual Development of Infants
Section 9.3 Helping Infants Learn

 Note Taking

Directions As you read, write notes, facts, and main ideas in the Note Taking column. Write key words and short phrases in the Cues column. Then summarize the section in the Summary box.

Cues	Note Taking
• responsiveness	**ENCOURAGING LEARNING** • Babies learn more and faster when their caregivers comfort, talk to, smile at, and play with them.
• play is children's work	**THE IMPORTANCE OF PLAY** • Playtime is essential for intellectual and physical development.

Summary
A baby needs a safe and stimulating environment for proper brain development.

Chapter 9

Chapter 9 Intellectual Development of Infants

Section 9.3 Helping Infants Learn

Mathematics
Purchasing Age-Appropriate Toys

Directions Suppose you have been given $100 to purchase age-appropriate toys for young children. Choose an age group for which you will buy toys. Go to a toy store, use a catalog, or use the Internet to research age-appropriate toys and their costs. Fill in the table with the age group you choose, the toys, the costs, and why they are appropriate for the age group. Do not forget to add the cost of all the toys.

> **NCTM Number and Operations** Understand numbers, ways of representing numbers, relationships among numbers, and number systems.

Age Groups
- 0 – 3 months
- 4 – 6 months
- 7 – 9 months
- 10 – 12 months

Age Group:

Toy	Cost	Why Appropriate
Total Cost:		

Chapter 9 Intellectual Development of Infants
Chapter Vocabulary

English Language Arts
Writing Sentences

> **NCTE 12** Use language to accomplish individual purposes.

Directions For each vocabulary word listed, write an original sentence that shows you understand its meaning. The first one is completed for you.

1. neuron Babies' brains develop links between nerve cells called neurons.
   _____

2. cortex _____
   _____

3. myelin _____
   _____

4. synapse _____
   _____

5. perception _____
   _____

6. attention span _____
   _____

7. concept _____
   _____

8. object permanence _____
   _____

9. symbolic thinking _____
   _____

10. childproof _____
    _____

Chapter 9

Chapter 10 Physical Development from One to Three

Section 10.1 Growth and Development from One to Three

Note Taking

Directions As you read, write notes, facts, and main ideas in the Note Taking column. Write key words and short phrases in the Cues column. Then summarize the section in the Summary box.

Cues	Note Taking
• heredity and environment	**GROWTH FROM ONE TO THREE** • Children ages 1 to 3 years change dramatically both in growth and development.
• general patterns of development	**DEVELOPMENT FROM ONE TO THREE** • General patterns of development—head to foot, near to far, and simple to complex—are evident in children ages 1 to 3.

Summary
Heredity plays a major role in child development.

Chapter 10

Chapter 10 Physical Development from One to Three

Section 10.1 Growth and Development from One to Three

English Language Arts
Summarizing Information

> **NCTE 6** Apply knowledge of language structure and conventions to discuss texts.

Directions Write a one-page summary of the information in Section 10.1, Growth and Development from One to Three. Be sure to check your summary for grammar and spelling errors.

_____

_____

_____

_____

_____

_____

_____

_____

_____

_____

_____

_____

_____

_____

_____

_____

_____

_____

_____

_____

_____

_____

_____

Chapter 10

Chapter 10 Physical Development from One to Three

Section 10.1 Growth and Development from One to Three

 Study Skills
Reading Comprehension

Directions Read the tips on developing reading comprehension. Then read the passage, circling unfamiliar words as you read. Finally, complete the activity. The first one is done for you.

Reading Comprehension Tips
• As you read, circle unfamiliar words.
• Write down the dictionary definition of unfamiliar words.
• Describe each definition in your own words.
• Think of a mental image for each word.
• Use each word in a sentence.

A Safe Environment

Childproofing a home is one way that parents create a safe environment for children. No home can be made safe for an unsupervised child, however. Children are impulsive. They have no idea about the result of their actions. Children, therefore, need monitoring. Young children need constant attention. Monitoring should not end entirely until children reach maturity. Even after children reach the teen years, parents need to know where they are and what they are doing because new threats emerge. Teens that are monitored show lower rates of drug and alcohol abuse, running away, and delinquency.

1. Word I circled _____ childproofing _____

   Dictionary definition _protecting a child from possible dangers_

   How I describe the word _making sure an area is safe so a child will not get hurt_

   My mental image of the word _baby near an electrical outlet with a cover_

   My sentence _Dan is childproofing his home because his daughter is beginning to crawl._

Activity continued on next page

Chapter 10 Physical Development from One to Three
Section 10.1 Growth and Development from One to Three

 Study Skills (continued)
Reading Comprehension

2. Word I circled _____

Dictionary definition _____

How I describe the word _____

My mental image of the word _____

My sentence _____

_____

3. Word I circled _____

Dictionary definition _____

How I describe the word _____

My mental image of the word _____

My sentence _____

_____

4. Word I circled _____

Dictionary definition _____

How I describe the word _____

My mental image of the word _____

My sentence _____

_____

5. Word I circled _____

Dictionary definition _____

How I describe the word _____

My mental image of the word _____

My sentence _____

_____

Chapter 10

Chapter 10 Physical Development from One to Three

Section 10.2 Caring for Children from One to Three

 Note Taking

Directions As you read, write notes, facts, and main ideas in the Note Taking column. Write key words and short phrases in the Cues column. Then summarize the section in the Summary box.

Cues	Note Taking
• sleep patterns	**SLEEPING** • Changes in sleep patterns are common in one- to three-year-olds.
• good eating habits	**NUTRITIONAL NEEDS AND EATING** • The eating habits and attitudes of one- to three-year-olds will influence their eating habits throughout life.
• medical checkups	**PHYSICAL HEALTH AND WELLNESS** • Parents and caregivers must keep children safe from accidents.
• self-dressing	**CLOTHING** • Clothing must be appropriate to allow children to dress and undress themselves.

Summary
Sleep disturbances affect some toddlers.

Chapter 10

Chapter 10 Physical Development from One to Three

Section 10.2 Caring for Children from One to Three

Mathematics
Convert Serving Sizes

> **NCTM Measurement** Understand measurable attributes of objects and the units, systems, and processes of measurement.

Directions Convert the fractions in the serving sizes below into decimals. Write your answers in the right column.

To convert fractions to decimals: Divide the numerator (the top number) by the denominator (the bottom number). If necessary, round your answer to the hundredths place (two places to the right of the decimal point). Example: Convert ⅕ to a decimal. 1 ÷ 5 = 0.2

Serving Sizes for Children Two and Three			
	Food	**Fraction**	**Decimal**
Milk Group	Milk, yogurt	½ cup	0.5 cup
	Frozen yogurt, pudding	¼ to ½ cup	
	Cheese	½ to 1 oz.	
Grain Group	Whole-grain bread	¼ to ½ slice	
	Ready-to-eat cereal	¼ to ⅓ cup	
	Spaghetti, rice, macaroni	¼ to ⅓ cup	
	Crackers	2 to 3	
	Hamburger bun	¼ to ½	
Meat and Beans Group	Egg	1	
	Chicken, hamburger, fish	1 to 2 oz.	
	Baked beans	¼ cup	
	Peanut butter	1 to 2 Tbsp.	
Vegetable Group	Carrots	¼ to ½	
	Corn, green beans, peas	¼ cup	
Fruit Group	Apple, banana	¼ to ½	
	Fruit juice	⅓ cup	
	Grapes, strawberries, peaches	¼ cup	

Chapter 10

Chapter 10 Physical Development from One to Three
Section 10.2 Caring for Children from One to Three

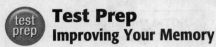 **Test Prep**
Improving Your Memory

Directions Use these tips to help you remember the information from your text. Then use content and academic vocabulary terms from this section to complete the sentences.

Improving Your Memory
• Focus on remembering what you are reading.
• Be alert when you read.
• Stop reading after one or two paragraphs, and ask yourself what you just read. Reread the paragraphs, if necessary.
• Relate the information to your life, if possible.
• Use your imagination to visualize, or see, the information as a picture in your mind's eye. Create pictures that are easy to remember.

1. Sometimes children's sleep is disturbed by __night terrors__ during the first few hours of sleep.

2. Often, children will not remember the disturbing _____.

3. _____ make our environment dirty.

4. Children must learn _____ such as using a tissue to wipe their nose and washing hands before eating.

5. Generally, at around 18 months, children are able to control their

   _____.

6. Clothing made from _____ is durable, wrinkle resistant, and quick-drying.

7. Children's sleepwear should be _____ so that it will not burn as quickly as other fabrics.

Chapter 10

Chapter 10 Physical Development from One to Three

Chapter Vocabulary

English Language Arts
Writing Articles

NCTE 12 Use language to accomplish individual purposes.

Directions Use the vocabulary terms below to write a newspaper article about a child's physical growth from ages one to three.

- toddler
- preschooler
- sensory integration
- developmentally appropriate
- dexterity
- variation
- proportion

_____

_____

_____

_____

_____

_____

_____

_____

_____

_____

_____

_____

_____

_____

_____

_____

_____

Chapter 10

Chapter 11 Emotional and Social Development from One to Three

Section 11.1 Emotional Development from One to Three

 Note Taking

Directions As you read, write notes, facts, and main ideas in the Note Taking column. Write key words and short phrases in the Cues column. Then summarize the section in the Summary box.

Cues	Note Taking
• experiences and temperament	**EMOTIONAL PATTERNS** • Emotional development goes in cycles in childhood.
• six basic emotions	**SPECIFIC EMOTIONS** • Even young babies have specific emotions.
• relationship's change	**EMOTIONAL ADJUSTMENT** • There are clear signs when a child and parents have a healthy relationship.
• adequate sleep	**SLEEP AND EMOTIONAL BEHAVIOR** • Sleep problems are one of the most common problems children experience.
Summary	
Children go through a series of emotional stages, both positive and somewhat negative.	

Name _____ Date _____ Class _____

Chapter 11 Emotional and Social Development from One to Three

Section 11.1 Emotional Development from One to Three

Science
Emotional Patterns of Young Children

NSES C Students should develop understanding of the interdependence of organisms; matter, energy, and organization in living systems; and behavior of organisms.

Directions Emotional patterns in children change dramatically from 18 months to three and one-half years. Read through the text, and record in the table the emotional patterns that are typical of children at each stage.

Emotional Patterns				
18 Months	**2 Years**	**2½ Years**	**3 Years**	**3½ Years**
Self-centered				

Chapter 11

Chapter 11 Emotional and Social Development from One to Three

Section 11.1 Emotional Development from One to Three

 Study Skills
Working in Teams

Directions The ability to work successfully as a member of a team is an important skill for a student and for an employee in the workplace. Study the ground rules for teamwork, then answer the questions.

Ground Rules for Teamwork
• Select roles for every team member appropriate to individual skills and interests.
• Take on your assigned role with a positive attitude.
• Contribute to the group by explaining your ideas and taking part in discussions.
• Schedule meeting times and stick to them.
• Share the workload equally.
• Respect the values and opinions of others.
• Encourage others to contribute their ideas.
• Value diversity.

1. Think of the different roles you might play when working on a team project. For each role, list three skills that would be useful in other areas of life.

   Spokesperson _public speaking, listening, writing, self-confidence_

   Recording secretary _____

   Project manager _____

   Editor _____

   Time keeper _____

2. Write a few sentences telling why it is important for team members to share the load equally, what can happen if they do not, and how to make sure everyone on a team contributes equally.

   _____

   _____

   _____

   _____

   _____

Chapter 11 Emotional and Social Development from One to Three

Section 11.2 Social Development from One to Three

 Note Taking

Directions As you read, write notes, facts, and main ideas in the Note Taking column. Write key words and short phrases in the Cues column. Then summarize the section in the Summary box.

Cues	Note Taking
• socialization	**GENERAL SOCIAL PATTERNS** • Young children gradually learn how to get along with other people.
• developing social skills	**MAKING FRIENDS** • The ability to make friends is important to normal social development.
• self-discipline	**GUIDING BEHAVIOR** • Guiding with understanding and firmness helps children learn self-discipline.

Summary
The socialization process involves gradually developing social skills and learning to get along with others.

Chapter 11

Chapter 11 Emotional and Social Development from One to Three

Section 11.2 Social Development from One to Three

Social Studies
Develop Social Skills

> **NCSS IV H Individual Development and Identity** Work cooperatively within groups and institutions to accomplish goals.

Directions Follow your teacher's directions to work with a partner or in a small group to develop a poster that shows ways parents and caregivers can help children develop social skills. Your poster should include words and illustrations. As you plan your work, be sure to divide tasks equally. Write down ideas for your poster.

Ideas for Poster

_____

_____

_____

_____

_____

_____

_____

_____

_____

_____

_____

_____

_____

_____

_____

_____

_____

Chapter 11 Emotional and Social Development from One to Three

Section 11.2 Social Development from One to Three

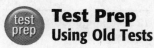 **Test Prep**
Using Old Tests

Directions Read the tips for using old tests to prepare for upcoming exams. Then answer the questions. The first one is done for you as an example.

Using Old Tests
• Review tests you have already taken for end-of-chapter or end-of-term tests. • Read any teacher's comments on the old tests. • Correct any questions you missed, and add the correct answers.

1. How does negativism affect the social relationships of two-and-one-half-year-olds?

A child may refuse to do things for some people.

_____

2. How is the play of a three-and-one-half-year-old different from that of younger children?

_____

_____

3. What harm is there in allowing children to spend all of their time with adults?

_____

_____

4. What are some ways to help toddlers develop good social skills?

_____

_____

5. How does guidance help children?

_____

_____

Name _____ Date _____ Class _____

Chapter 11 Emotional and Social Development from One to Three

Chapter Vocabulary

 English Language Arts
Fill in the Blank

> **NCTE 12** Use language to accomplish individual purposes.

Directions For each blank in the article below, write the vocabulary term that makes the most sense.

- autonomy
- cooperative play
- negativism
- parallel play
- phobias
- self-centered

- self-concept
- self-discipline
- separation anxiety
- socialization
- temper tantrums

---

1. Eighteen-month-old children are typically _____self-centered_____ and are known for their _____. Children in this age group are also known for their _____.

2. Children often develop _____ such as fear of the dark. Another common fear is _____, or the fear of being away from parent, care-givers, or the normal environment. Children often outgrow these fears. Parents can help children deal with their fears.

3. As they grow, children become more aware of their individual differences. The individual traits that make them special become part of their _____, which is how people see themselves. Children who see themselves as good and capable have a positive self-concept.

4. Young children gradually learn how to get along with other people, first in their own family, then with people in other groups. The process of learning to get along with others is called _____.

5. Eighteen-month-old children usually do not play together. They engage in _____ in which they play near but not with another child. By the time children reach three years of age they typically engage in _____, in which they play and interact with others.

6. Guidance is important in developing children's behavior. It can help children learn _____, or control of their own behavior. Guidance can also help children develop _____, or independence.

Name _____ Date _____ Class _____

Chapter 12 Intellectual Development from One to Three

Section 12.1 Brain Development from One to Three

 Note Taking

Directions As you read, write notes, facts, and main ideas in the Note Taking column. Write key words and short phrases in the Cues column. Then summarize the section in the Summary box.

Cues	Note Taking
• neuroscience	**BRAIN DEVELOPMENT** • The brain plays a major role in directing behavior and determining intelligence.
• incidental learning	**METHODS OF LEARNING** • Much of what children learn comes from everyday experiences and play.
• attention	**INTELLECTUAL ACTIVITY AREAS** • The seven areas of intellectual activity develop throughout life.

Summary
Intelligence is determined by heredity and environment.

Chapter 12

Chapter 12 Intellectual Development from One to Three

Section 12.1 Brain Development from One to Three

 Social Studies
Heredity and Environment

Directions Imagine that you work for a local newspaper and have been asked to write an article that explains how heredity and environment help to shape intelligence. Use the space to write a three-paragraph article.

> **NCSS IV D Individual Development and Identity** Apply concepts, methods, and theories about the study of human growth and development, such as learning, and perception.

_____

_____

_____

_____

_____

_____

_____

_____

_____

_____

_____

_____

_____

_____

_____

_____

_____

_____

_____

_____

_____

Chapter 12 Intellectual Development from One to Three

Section 12.1 Brain Development from One to Three

 Study Skills
Improving Listening Skills

Directions Read the tips on how to improve your listening skills. Then answer the questions that follow.

Improving Your Listening Skills
• Before the speaker begins speaking, skim any written material that has been provided to prepare you for listening.   • Try to anticipate what the speaker is going to say. You may not always be correct, but this anticipation will prepare your brain to receive new information.   • Try to relate new material you hear to something in your life. This can help you to better understand what you are hearing when a speaker is talking.   • Take notes while you are listening. Afterward, rewrite your notes and study them. Restate what you heard in your own words.

1. How does anticipating what the speaker is going to say before you hear it help you listen?
   It helps prepare your brain to receive new information.
   _____

2. What is one way to better understand what you are hearing when a speaker is talking?
   _____
   _____

3. What should you do while the speaker is speaking?
   _____
   _____

4. What should you do after the speaker has finished speaking?
   _____
   _____

5. What advice would you give another student about listening actively?
   _____
   _____

Chapter 12

Chapter 12 Intellectual Development from One to Three

Section 12.2 Encouraging Learning from One to Three

 Note Taking

Directions As you read, write notes, facts, and main ideas in the Note Taking column. Write key words and short phrases in the Cues column. Then summarize the section in the Summary box.

Cues	Note Taking
• reading readiness	**READINESS FOR LEARNING** • Children need to have acquired certain skills before they are ready to read or learn basic math concepts.
• inborn ability	**LANGUAGE ABILITIES** • From one to three years of age, children's language skills grow rapidly.
• play affects motor skills and social skills	**PLAY ACTIVITIES AND TOYS** • Toys play an important role in the development of one- to three-year-olds.

Summary
Parents and caregivers can encourage reading and math readiness during play and everyday activities.

Chapter 12

Chapter 12 Intellectual Development from One to Three

Section 12.2 Encouraging Learning from One to Three

 Mathematics
Math Readiness

> NCTM Problem Solving Monitor and reflect on the process of problem solving.

Directions Think about the activities you do or places you go every day. How could you use these activities or places to help a child develop skills needed for math readiness? Create two examples of math readiness activities for young children. Examples should come from everyday activities.

_____

_____

_____

_____

_____

_____

_____

_____

_____

_____

_____

_____

_____

_____

_____

_____

_____

Chapter 12

Chapter 12 Intellectual Development from One to Three

Section 12.2 Encouraging Learning from One to Three

 Test Prep
Preparing for Tests

Directions Read the tips for preparing for tests. Then answer the questions below. The first one is done for you as an example.

Preparing for Tests
• Start preparing for tests on the first day of class. • At the end of each day, review what you learned by reading your notes and asking yourself questions about the material. Reread any sections of the text you do not understand well. • At the end of each week, review what you have learned. • Review for several short periods instead of one long period so you will be more rested when you study. • Turn the main points into questions, and answer the questions.

1. What are two main points in Section 12.2?
   Children need to have certain skills before they are ready to read or learn basic
   _____
   math concepts. Toys play an important role in children's development.
   _____

2. What part of Section 12.2 should you re-read for better understanding? Explain the section in your own words.
   _____
   _____
   _____

3. Why would it be helpful for you to study Section 12.2 in short periods of time rather than long periods of time?
   _____
   _____
   _____

4. Turn this heading into a question: Readiness for Learning. Then answer the question.
   _____
   _____
   _____

5. Turn this heading into a question: Speech Difficulties. Then answer the question.
   _____
   _____
   _____

Chapter 12 Intellectual Development from One to Three

Chapter Vocabulary

English Language Atrs
Build a Word Search

> **NCTE 12** Use language to accomplish individual purposes.

Directions Use the vocabulary terms to create your own word-search puzzle. Carefully write each term in the squares of the grid, one letter per box. Arrange the terms going up, down, across, diagonally, or backward. Do not include hyphens or spaces. Fill in the remaining squares with random letters. Then exchange and solve the puzzles with a classmate.

Content Vocabulary		Academic Vocabulary
• neuroscience	• creativity	• elicit
• intelligence	• reading readiness	• stifle
• incidental learning	• math readiness	• unstructured
• trial-and-error learning	• articulation	• decipher
• imitation	• stuttering	
• directed learning		

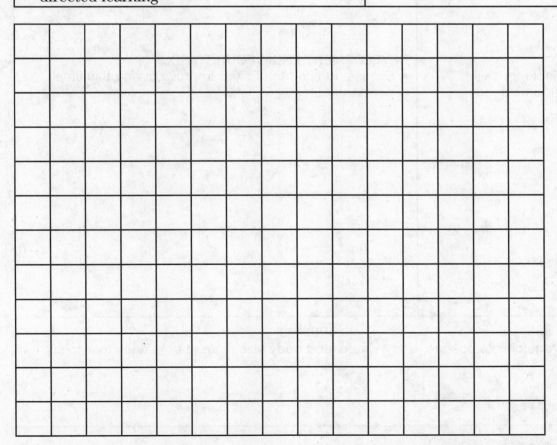

Chapter 13 Physical Development from Four to Six
Section 13.1 Growth and Development from Four to Six

 Note Taking

Directions As you read, write notes, facts, and main ideas in the Note Taking column. Write key words and short phrases in the Cues column. Then summarize the section in the Summary box.

Cues	Note Taking
• practice makes perfect	**GROWTH FROM FOUR TO SIX** • Children from ages four to six are always improving their physical skills.
• timetable for skill development	**DEVELOPMENT FROM FOUR TO SIX** • Gross and fine motor skills improve during this time period.

Summary

An average child's posture, body shape, and body size change from ages four to six.

Chapter 13

Chapter 13 Physical Development from Four to Six
Section 13.1 Growth and Development from Four to Six

 English Language Arts
Characteristics of Four- to Six-Year-Olds

> **NCTE 7** Conduct research and gather, evaluate, and synthesize data to communicate discoveries.

Directions Choose one of the listed characteristics of four- to six-year-olds. Use a minimum of three resources to research this characteristic. Write a one-page report to share your findings. Be sure to cite the three sources you use during your research. Your report should be written in standard English and should not contain grammar or spelling errors. Use this page to jot down notes for your report.

Characteristics of Four- to Six-Year-Olds

- height
- weight
- posture
- body shape
- teeth
- gross motor skills
- fine motor skills
- hand preference

_____

_____

_____

_____

_____

_____

_____

_____

_____

_____

_____

_____

_____

_____

_____

_____

Chapter 13

Chapter 13 Physical Development from Four to Six
Section 13.1 Growth and Development from Four to Six

Study Skills
Identify Learning Styles

Directions Read the tips on identifying your learning styles and answer the questions.

Tips for Identifying Learning Styles
• Think about things you have learned and how you learned them. For example, did you learn by reading, looking at pictures, or listening to someone speak? Try to identify the ways in which you learn best.
• Experiment with a variety of learning strategies to help you identify your learning styles. For example, you might read especially challenging text aloud to help you hear text as you study. This strategy may help you if you are a verbal/linguistic learner, which is a learner who learns best by saying, hearing, or seeing words.

1. Name something you have learned to do, and explain how you learned to do it.

   _____

   _____

   _____

   _____

2. How might experimenting with learning strategies help you improve your learning skills?

   _____

   _____

   _____

   _____

3. List some learning strategies you will try to help you determine your preferred learning styles.

   _____

   _____

   _____

   _____

Chapter 13

Chapter 13 Physical Development from Four to Six

Section 13.2 Caring for Children from Four to Six

 Note Taking

Directions As you read, write notes, facts, and main ideas in the Note Taking column. Write key words and short phrases in the Cues column. Then summarize the section in the Summary box.

Cues	Note Taking
• MyPyramid	**HEALTH AND WELLNESS** • Good nutrition is essential for children ages four to six.
• dressing and choosing clothes	**SELF-CARE SKILLS** • There are many ways four- to six-year-olds can help care for themselves.
• sleep needs	**SLEEPING AND TOILETING** • Caregivers need to set an appropriate bedtime.
• safety concerns	**OUTDOOR SAFETY** • Children ages four to six spend much of their time playing outside.

Summary
The eating habits children establish influence the eating habits and health they experience as adults.

Chapter 13

Chapter 13 Physical Development from Four to Six

Section 13.2 Caring for Children from Four to Six

Science
Physical Activity Schedule

> **NSES F** Students should develop understanding of personal and community health.

Directions Use the table below to plan a two-week physical activity schedule for four- to six-year-olds. Activities should be age-appropriate and last for 30 minutes.

Physical Activity Schedule		
Day	**Week 1**	**Week 2**
Monday	Use playground equipment	
Tuesday		
Wednesday		
Thursday		
Friday		
Saturday		
Sunday		

Name _____ Date _____ Class _____

Chapter 13 Physical Development from Four to Six

Section 13.2 Caring for Children from Four to Six

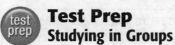 **Test Prep**
Studying in Groups

Directions Read the information about preparing for group study, then answer the questions.

Preparing for Group Study
• Ask two or three people to study with you.
• Schedule enough time for your group to cover all the material you will be studying. Make sure there is time for questions and discussion.
• Have one member of the group act as leader to keep everyone focused.
• Before the group meets, the leader should assign sections of the text to each member. Members should then write questions covering their assigned text selection.
• At the meeting, take turns asking and answering the questions. If everyone can answer a question, move on to the next question. Put aside any questions that someone cannot answer and ask them again later.
• Be prepared. Make it clear to all members of the group that they need to be ready with their questions and be able to answer questions on the text.
• Plan for a short social time before and after the meeting. Take at least one short break. The group leader should keep track of the time to get everyone focused after breaks.

Chapter 13

1. Why do you need a group leader?

   _____

   _____

2. Why should you plan for short breaks?

   _____

   _____

3. Why is it important for everyone to be prepared before the group meets?

   _____

   _____

4. What advice would you give someone who wanted to get a group together to prepare for a test?

   _____

   _____

Chapter 13 Physical Development from Four to Six
Chapter Vocabulary

English Language Arts
Visual Descriptions

NCTE 12 Use language to accomplish individual purposes.

Directions Write a description of a visual representation that will help you remember the vocabulary terms. The first one is completed for you.

1. permanent teeth an adult with a broad smile showing many teeth
   _____

2. ambidextrous _____
   _____

3. group identification _____
   _____

4. fluoride _____
   _____

5. enamel _____
   _____

6. erect _____
   _____

7. dexterity _____
   _____

8. persuade _____
   _____

9. undermine _____
   _____

Chapter 14 Emotional and Social Development from Four to Six

Section 14.1 Emotional Development from Four to Six

 Note Taking

Directions As you read, write notes, facts, and main ideas in the Note Taking column. Write key words and short phrases in the Cues column. Then summarize the section in the Summary box.

Cues	Note Taking
• independence	**EMOTIONAL PATTERNS** • Independence is a characteristic that marks emotional development at ages four to six.
• anger	**SPECIFIC EMOTIONS** • As children grow older they feel and express emotions more, and learn to control their emotions.
• show respect	**SELF-CONFIDENCE** • Dealing with unfamiliar situations and learning new skills increases self-confidence.

Summary
There are a number of characteristics that mark the emotional development of four- to six-year-olds.

Chapter 14

Chapter 14 Emotional and Social Development from Four to Six

Section 14.1 Emotional Development from Four to Six

English Language Arts
Reducing Worry and Stress

| NCTE 4 Use written language to communicate effectively. |

Directions Use information from the text to create a brochure that describes ways parents and caregivers can help children reduce worry and tension. You might start with the title of your brochure in panel 1. Use illustrations when possible. Proofread your brochure and correct any spelling or grammar errors. Use the space below to plan your brochure.

1 Left Inside Panel	2 Middle Inside Panel	3 Right Inside Panel

4 Inside Flap	5 Back Panel	6 Front Cover

Chapter 14 Emotional and Social Development from Four to Six

Section 14.1 Emotional Development from Four to Six

Study Skills
Preparing for Class

Directions Follow these general tips on preparing for class. Then complete the questions by filling in each blank with the correct term.

Tips to Prepare for Class
• Come to class with your homework completed.
• Skim any material you have read to prepare for today.
• Review your notes from the previous lecture.
• Talk to your teacher about any problems you are having with the material.

Word List

- anger
- fear
- impulsive
- initiative
- jealousy
- self-confidence
- tension
- turmoil
- worry

1. Many six-year-olds experience extreme confusion and agitation, or _____.

2. Emotional stress is also known as _____.

3. Five-year-olds' actions are often _____. They act spontaneously and do not consider the consequences of their actions.

4. Sibling rivalry, or _____, is common in four- to six-year-olds.

5. Preschoolers begin to take _____ and make decisions on their own.

6. _____ often causes six-year-olds to be hurtful with words. They tease, insult, nag, and make fun of others.

7. There are many ways in which parents and other caregivers can help preschoolers and kindergarteners develop _____.

8. Children may _____ about everything from a fire in their home, to a stranger stealing them, to a bully in the neighborhood or at school.

9. Imagination is a major emotional force in children from four to six, and often their _____ centers on imaginary dangers.

Chapter 14

Chapter 14 Emotional and Social Development from Four to Six

Section 14.2 Social and Moral Development from Four to Six

 Note Taking

Directions As you read, write notes, facts, and main ideas in the Note Taking column. Write key words and short phrases in the Cues column. Then summarize the section in the Summary box.

Cues	Note Taking
• interacting with new people	**GENERAL SOCIAL PATTERNS** • Before entering school, children must learn specific, important social skills.
• moral development	**MORAL DEVELOPMENT** • Moral development is the process of learning to base one's behavior on beliefs about what is right and wrong.
• talk about feelings	**RESOLVING CONFLICTS** • Children need to learn that aggressive behavior is not acceptable.
Summary The world for children from ages four to six expands dramatically as they begin school.	

Chapter 14 Emotional and Social Development from Four to Six

Section 14.2 Social and Moral Development from Four to Six

Social Studies
Teaching Moral Development

NCSS IV F Individual Development and Identity Analyze the role of perceptions, attitudes, values, and beliefs in the development of personal identity.

Directions Create some scenarios in which four- to six-year-olds are taught moral development. After you write the scenarios, explain how morals are taught in each scenario. The first one is done for you.

Scenario 1: Four-year-old Geof and his mother are in the grocery store when Geof takes a cookie out of the bakery case and stuffs it in his mouth before his mother can stop him. His mother tells him that is stealing, he must pay for the food in the grocery store before eating it. Explanation: Geof's mother teaches him about stealing.

Scenario 2: _____

_____

_____

_____

Scenario 3: _____

_____

_____

_____

Scenario 4: _____

_____

_____

_____

_____

Chapter 14

Chapter 14 Emotional and Social Development from Four to Six

Section 14.2 Social and Moral Development from Four to Six

Test Prep
Using Flash Cards

Directions Follow the directions to make flash cards that you can use as study aids.

- Use 3-inch by 5-inch index cards.
- Create questions from headings, key words, end-of-section questions, end-of-chapter questions, and any questions in the text. Write your question on one side of the index card. See the sample.
- On the back of the index card, write the answer to the question.
- Review the cards in random order. Look at the front of the card. Read the questions aloud. Then answer the question.
- Turn the card over to review the answer.

Front of Card

What are five ways to help children reduce worry and tension?

Back of Card

- Look for the cause.
- Give children time to calm down.
- Provide chances to get rid of tension.
- Read a book about the issue causing stress.
- Maintain normal limits on behavior.

Chapter 14 Emotional and Social Development from Four to Six

Chapter Vocabulary

 English Language Arts
Matching Definitions

NCTE 12 Use language to accomplish individual purposes.

Directions Write the correct vocabulary term on the line next to its definition.

- aggressive behavior
- competition
- impulsive
- initiative
- moral development
- peer
- refine
- resort
- self-confidence
- tension
- turmoil

1. _____ improve

2. _____ the motivation to accomplish more

3. _____ someone close to one's own age

4. _____ the process of learning to base one's behavior on beliefs about what is right and wrong

5. _____ belief in one's own abilities

6. _____ a state of extreme confusion or agitation

7. _____ choose

8. _____ to act spontaneously

9. _____ emotional stress

10. _____ rivalry with the goal of winning or outperforming others

11. _____ hostile, and at times destructive behavior that people display when faced with conflict

Chapter 15 Intellectual Development from Four to Six

Section 15.1 Brain Development from Four to Six

 Note Taking

Directions As you read, write notes, facts, and main ideas in the Note Taking column. Write key words and short phrases in the Cues column. Then summarize the section in the Summary box.

Cues	Note Taking
• intelligence quotient (IQ)	**WHAT IS INTELLIGENCE?** • Intelligence tests are composed of tasks and questions that correspond to what is expected of children of various ages.
• intelligence increases	**INTELLECTUAL DEVELOPMENT** • Researchers have identified intellectual skills commonly seen in children ages four to six.

Summary
Intelligence quotient (IQ) tests must be used with caution.

Chapter 15

Chapter 15 Intellectual Development from Four to Six

Section 15.1 Brain Development from Four to Six

 Science
Survey of Eight Intelligences

> **NSES A** Students should develop understandings about scientific inquiry.

Directions Create a survey like the one below. Distribute your survey to classmates, parents, and friends. Ask participants to rank their own intelligences from weakest to strongest, with 8 being the strongest. After you have collected your data, create a table like the one on the next page. Fill in the table based on the data you collect. Write a brief analysis and report of your results on a separate piece of paper.

Multiple Intelligences Survey	
Intelligence	**Ranking from 1–8**
Linguistic involves sensitivity to language, the ability to learn languages, and the ability to use language to accomplish goals.	
Logical-mathematical consists of the ability to analyze problems using logic, perform mathematical operations, and explore issues scientifically.	
Spatial involves an understanding of the potential use of space, thinking in three-dimensional terms, and imagining things in clear visual images.	
Musical involves skill in performing, composing, and appreciating musical patterns.	
Bodily-kinesthetic has to do with the potential to use one's body to solve problems, and using the mind to coordinate body movements.	
Interpersonal involves the potential to understand the intentions, desires, and motivations of others.	
Intrapersonal implies the capacity to understand oneself, including fears, hopes, and motivations.	
Naturalist involves recognizing, categorizing, and drawing upon the features of the environment.	

Activity continued on next page

Chapter 15

Chapter 15 Intellectual Development from Four to Six

Section 15.1 Brain Development from Four to Six

Science (continued)
Survey of Eight Intelligences

Intelligences	% Ranked #1	% Ranked #2	% Ranked #3	% Ranked #4	% Ranked #5	% Ranked #6	% Ranked #7	% Ranked #8
Linguistic								
Logical-mathematical								
Spatial								
Musical								
Bodily-kinesthetic								
Interpersonal								
Intrapersonal								
Naturalist								

Chapter 15

Chapter 15 Intellectual Development from Four to Six

Section 15.1 Brain Development from Four to Six

 Study Skills
Paying Attention in the Classroom

Directions Use these general tips on paying attention in the classroom to help you better focus on the information that you will learn in class. Use complete sentences to answer the questions.

Tips to Help You Pay Attention in the Classroom
• Resist distractions by sitting in the front of the room and by focusing on the instructor through active listening and note taking. • Ask questions for clarification when you are having trouble understanding the material. • Train yourself to avoid distractions such as persons entering or exiting the room. Keep your concentration on what is being taught.

1. What can be said about a child with an IQ score of 100?
According to the Stanford-Binet test, the child is of average intelligence.

2. Why should we not rely on intelligence tests to rank a child's mental ability?

_____

_____

_____

3. Name the eight intelligences identified by psychologist Howard Gardner.

_____

_____

_____

4. During the preoperational period, how do children view the world?

_____

_____

_____

5. According to Vygotsky's theory, how does learning take place?

_____

_____

_____

Chapter 15

Chapter 15 Intellectual Development from Four to Six

Section 15.2 Learning from Four to Six

 Note Taking

Directions As you read, write notes, facts, and main ideas in the Note Taking column. Write key words and short phrases in the Cues column. Then summarize the section in the Summary box.

Cues	Note Taking
	HELP CHILDREN LEARN
• everyday experiences	• Parents and caregivers can encourage children's enthusiasm for learning.
	SPEECH DEVELOPMENT
• vocabulary	• As children get older, their vocabularies widen and sentences grow more complex.
	THE SCHOOL EXPERIENCE
• preschool	• Many parents place children in preschool so they can adjust to a school setting.

Summary
Experiences form the basis for children's learning.

Chapter 15 Intellectual Development from Four to Six

Section 15.2 Learning from Four to Six

 Mathematics
Purchasing Art Supplies

> **NCTM Numbers and Operations** Compute fluently and make reasonable estimates.

Directions Imagine that you have $50 to spend on art supplies for three four- to six-year-old children. Look in catalogs and online to find appropriate art supplies and their costs. Fill in the chart below with the information you find. Total your costs and make sure they do not go over $50.

Art Supplies	Cost
Total Cost	

Chapter 15

Chapter 15 Intellectual Development from Four to Six

Section 15.2 Learning from Four to Six

 Test Prep
Test-Taking Checklist

Directions Read the test-taking tips. Then answer the questions.

Test-Taking
• Make sure each question has an answer. • Proofread the short-answer and essay questions for any grammar or spelling errors. • Include all the important details on the short-answer and essay questions.

1. How can helping around the house be a learning experience for four- to six-year-old children?

   _____

   _____

2. Why is it important to develop an early interest in reading?

   _____

   _____

3. What is alliteration?

   _____

   _____

4. Why is it important to talk to children about their art work?

   _____

   _____

5. What can parents do to assess whether their child is ready for school?

   _____

   _____

6. List three behaviors of a child that is ready for school.

   _____

   _____

Chapter 15

Chapter 15 Intellectual Development from Four to Six

Chapter Vocabulary

English Language Arts
Graphic Organizers

NCTE 12 Use language to accomplish individual purposes.

Directions Follow the steps to fill in the graphic organizer.

1. Read the terms in the first column.

2. Write what you think the terms mean in the second column.

3. Use a dictionary to learn the definitions of the terms and write them in the third column.

Term	Predict what the term means	Write the dictionary definition
intelligence quotient	intelligence score	a numerical score that indicates whether a person's intelligence is average or above or below average for his or her age
cultural bias		
multiple intelligences		
phoneme		
alliteration		
bilingual		
finger play		
regulate		
oriented		

Chapter 15

Chapter 16 Physical Development from Seven to Twelve

Section 16.1 Growth and Development from Seven to Twelve

 Note Taking

Directions As you read, write notes, facts, and main ideas in the Note Taking column. Write key words and short phrases in the Cues column. Then summarize the section in the Summary box.

Cues	Note Taking
• physical changes	**GROWTH FROM SEVEN TO TWELVE** • Children's bodies begin to take on the physical characteristics of adulthood.
• muscle strength	**MOTOR SKILLS** • From ages seven to twelve, motor skills improve rapidly.

Summary
From the ages of seven to twelve, children go through a period of profound physical change.

Chapter 16 Physical Development from Seven to Twelve

Section 16.1 Growth and Development from Seven to Twelve

 Science
Time Line of Changes

> **NSES C** Develop understanding of the behavior of organisms.

Directions Fill in the time line with the physical changes that occur in boys and girls at 7 to 12 years old. Answers will cover ranges of ages. One of the answers is provided.

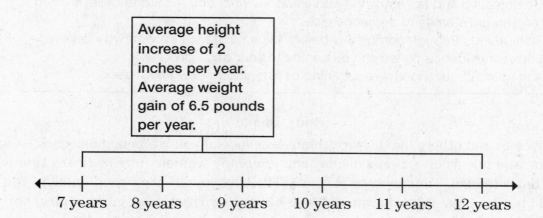

Chapter 16 Physical Development from Seven to Twelve

Section 16.1 Growth and Development from Seven to Twelve

 Study Skills
Critical Thinking

Directions Thinking critically is important when taking in new material and information. Practice these tips for improving your critical thinking skills as you read the article about body image. Then answer the questions.

Tips for Improving Critical Thinking Skills
• Be objective and honest with yourself about what you think and believe when reading or listening to someone else. • Think things through completely before taking a stance on what you believe. • Look for evidence on which you can base your decisions. • Ask yourself questions while reading or listening to new information.

Body Image

Our society and others like it favor thinness, especially in women. Magazines, newspapers, and television screens display camera-ready women, unrealistically thin with their flaws hidden. The message is clear: "The way you are isn't good enough. You should become like the cover model who doesn't sweat, doesn't grow hair on her slender legs, and has a flat stomach, perfect face, and small feet. She is also perfectly happy. If you are not perfectly happy, it is because your body is not perfect by these standards." Acceptance of such unreasonable standards has driven many young women in our society to be obsessed with thinness.

1. How do you think the author of this article feels about the media's portrayal of women?

   _____

   _____

2. What do you think the author means by "unreasonable standards"?

   _____

   _____

3. Do you agree or disagree with the author of this article? Explain your answer.

   _____

   _____

Chapter 16 Physical Development from Seven to Twelve

Section 16.2 Caring for Children from Seven to Twelve

 Note Taking

Directions As you read, write notes, facts, and main ideas in the Note Taking column. Write key words and short phrases in the Cues column. Then summarize the section in the Summary box.

Cues	Note Taking
• Dietary Guidelines for Americans	**NUTRITION** • Dietary Guidelines for Americans presents a comprehensive plan for incorporating nutritious food and physical activity into daily life.
• physical fitness	**PHYSICAL HEALTH AND WELLNESS** • Being physically active can greatly increase overall health.

Summary

During middle childhood and the preteen years, children experience tremendous physical and emotional growth.

Chapter 16 Physical Development from Seven to Twelve

Section 16.2 Caring for Children from Seven to Twelve

Mathematics
One-Week Menu

> **NCTM Problem Solving** Solve problems that arise in mathematics and in other contexts.

Directions Use the Dietary Guidelines for Americans and MyPyramid to create a nutritious one-week menu for children ages seven to twelve. Be sure the menu includes all of the daily recommendations and includes a variety of foods.

	Breakfast	Snack	Lunch	Snack	Dinner
Monday					
Tuesday					
Wednesday					
Thursday					
Friday					
Saturday					
Sunday					

Chapter 16 Physical Development from Seven to Twelve

Section 16.2 Caring for Children from Seven to Twelve

 Test Prep
Preparing for Open-Book Tests

Directions Read the information about preparing for open-book tests.
Then answer the questions.

Preparing for Open-Book Tests
• Keep up-to-date on reading the text and reviewing your notes. You may use both the text and your notes in an open-book test.   • Put sticky notes in the margins of your text next to important points you want to remember. Write key words and phrases on the sticky notes.   • Use different colors of highlighter to mark your notes. You might try orange for important dates, yellow for key words and their definitions, and pink for major ideas. When your eye scans your notes, you can find the information quickly by the color.   • Organize and edit the notes that you want to take with you to the test. Do not overburden yourself with too many notes. You will have a limited amount of time to take the test, so get organized. Make sure you can find everything you need quickly.

1. What materials can you use in an open-book test?

   _____

   _____

2. How can sticky notes help you?

   _____

   _____

3. How would highlighting your notes with different colors help you?

   _____

   _____

4. Why is organization prior to the test important?

   _____

   _____

5. Would you tell another student that an open-book test is easier or harder than a closed-book test? Explain your answer.

   _____

   _____

Chapter 16 Physical Development from Seven to Twelve

Chapter Vocabulary

English Language Arts
Writing Sentences

NCTE 12 Use language to accomplish individual purposes.

Directions Write a sentence for each word that shows you understand its meaning. The first one is completed for you.

1. growth spurt Jeremy experienced a growth spurt over the summer so he was two inches taller when he went back to school in the fall.

2. puberty _____

_____

3. scoliosis _____

_____

4. body image _____

_____

5. eating disorder _____

_____

6. fiber _____

_____

7. MyPyramid _____

_____

8. sedentary activity _____

_____

9. sealant _____

_____

10. orthodontist _____

_____

Chapter 17 Emotional and Social Development from Seven to Twelve

Section 17.1 Emotional Development from Seven to Twelve

 Note Taking

Directions As you read, write notes, facts, and main ideas in the Note Taking column. Write key words and short phrases in the Cues column. Then summarize the section in the Summary box.

Cues	Note Taking
• 7- to 10-year-olds progressions	**EMOTIONAL CHANGES** • Children ages 7 to 10 progress from negative to positive, unhappiness to happiness, and gain independence and self-confidence.
• controlling emotions	**SPECIFIC EMOTIONS** • Children gradually gain emotional control.
• unique personality	**A SENSE OF SELF** • Sense of self is your idea of who you are based on emotions, personality, and perception of the world.

Summary
Children ages 7 to 12 may sometimes feel that they are on an emotional roller coaster.

Chapter 17

Name _____ Date _____ Class _____

Chapter 17 Emotional and Social Development from Seven to Twelve

Section 17.1 Emotional Development from Seven to Twelve

 Social Studies
Charting Emotional Change

NCSS IV C Individual Development and Identity Describe the ways family, religion, gender, and other group and cultural influences contribute to the development of a sense of self.

Directions Fill in the flowchart with the emotional changes that occur for each age listed. The first one has been completed for you. Then, on the lines at the bottom of the page, explain how these changes affect a child's sense of self.

Seven-year-olds: withdrawn and quiet; stay close to home; worry a great deal; may not want to talk about feelings; sensitive to what others say about them

⬇

Eight-year-olds:

⬇

Nine-year-olds:

⬇

Ten-year-olds:

⬇

Preteens:

_____

_____

_____

_____

_____

_____

_____

_____

Chapter 17

Chapter 17 Emotional and Social Development from Seven to Twelve

Section 17.1 Emotional Development from Seven to Twelve

 Study Skills
Creating a Topic Web

Directions Topic webs are a good way to organize information about a subject. You can create a different topic web for each concept you have studied. Then you can use the topic webs to study and recall related information. For this exercise, the topic name "Developing a Sense of Competence" is in the center circle. Write an idea or fact related to the topic in each outlying circle. The first one is done for you.

Chapter 17

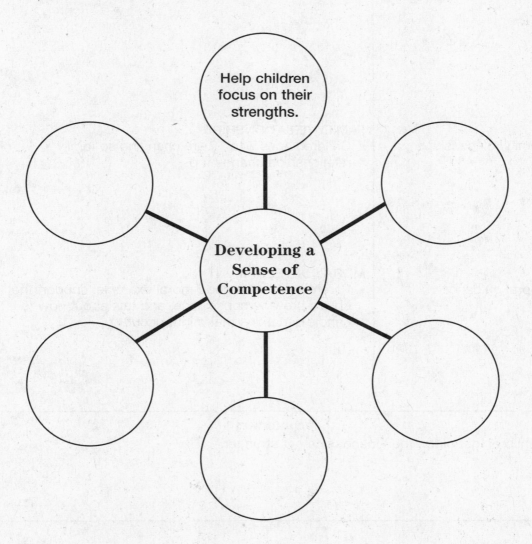

Chapter 17 Emotional and Social Development from Seven to Twelve

Section 17.2 Social and Moral Development from Seven to Twelve

 Note Taking

Directions As you read, write notes, facts, and main ideas in the Note Taking column. Write key words and short phrases in the Cues column. Then summarize the section in the Summary box.

Cues	Note Taking
• qualities of friends	**RELATIONSHIPS WITH PEERS** • Children ages 7 to 12 often look for loyalty, trustworthiness, kindness, and fun in their friends.
• family relationships	**FAMILY RELATIONSHIPS** • Children ages 7 to 12 are changing so family relationships change too.
• moral guidance	**MORAL DEVELOPMENT** • Parents can set a good moral example, support the child's growing conscience, and talk about how to handle situations that might occur.

Summary
As children get older, their friendships get stronger.

Chapter 17

Chapter 17 Emotional and Social Development from Seven to Twelve

Section 17.2 Social and Moral Development from Seven to Twelve

 English Language Arts
Advice Column

> **NCTE 12** Use language to accomplish individual purposes.

Directions Use the space below to write an advice column for parents of 7- to 12-year-olds. Your advice should give parents suggestions for how to help them guide their child's moral development.

Dear Parents of 7- to 12-Year-Olds:

_____

_____

_____

_____

_____

_____

_____

_____

_____

_____

_____

_____

_____

_____

_____

_____

_____

_____

_____

_____

_____

_____

Chapter 17

Chapter 17 Emotional and Social Development from Seven to Twelve

Section 17.2 Social and Moral Development from Seven to Twelve

 Test Prep
Concept Maps

Directions Organizing information in concept maps is a good way to study for tests. Practice using concept maps by using the information from the reading passage to fill in the concept map. Look for relationships among the details in the passage.

Handling Negative Peer Pressure

Learning to handle peer pressure is a major task of the teen years. When you want to be part of the group, walking away may not be easy, especially for the sake of a principle.

What kind of person can actually stand up to negative pressures? First, you need a clear vision of what you believe. You also need to be willing to let your convictions show. You need the confidence to take a stand and not let others' reactions bother you. Finally, you have to want the satisfaction that comes when you do what you truly believe is right and is best for you and others.

Standing Up to Negative Peer Pressure

Chapter 17 Emotional and Social Development from Seven to Twelve

Chapter Vocabulary

 English Language Arts
Fill in the Blank

> **NCTE 12** Use language to accomplish individual purposes.

Directions Fill in the circle next to the word or phrase that best completes the sentence.

Content Vocabulary	
• anxiety	• bullying
• sense of self	• peer pressure
• sense of competence	• conformity
• gender identity	

1. _____ is a social group's influence on the way individuals behave.
   - ● Peer pressure   ○ Conformity
   - ○ Sense of self   ○ Gender identity

2. _____ means directing aggression or abuse toward another person, usually someone weaker.
   - ○ Anxiety   ○ Bullying
   - ○ Conformity   ○ Peer pressure

3. _____ means being like one another.
   - ○ Peer pressure   ○ Conformity
   - ○ Sense of self   ○ Gender identity

4. _____ is the feeling that one can be successful and meet most challenges.
   - ○ Conformity   ○ Sense of self
   - ○ Sense of competence   ○ Gender identity

5. _____ is your idea of who you are, based on your emotions, personality, and the ways you perceive the world.
   - ○ Peer pressure   ○ Conformity
   - ○ Sense of self   ○ Gender identity

6. _____ is a state of uncertainty and fear, often about an unspecified but seemingly immediate threat.
   - ○ Anxiety   ○ Bullying
   - ○ Conformity   ○ Peer pressure

7. _____ is the awareness of being male or female.
   - ○ Conformity   ○ Sense of self
   - ○ Sense of competence   ○ Gender identity

Chapter 17

Chapter 18 Intellectual Development from Seven to Twelve

Section 18.1 Brain Development from Seven to Twelve

Note Taking

Directions As you read, write notes, facts, and main ideas in the Note Taking column. Write key words and short phrases in the Cues column. Then summarize the section in the Summary box.

Cues	Note Taking
• brain is center of learning	**SIGNS OF INCREASED INTELLECTUAL GROWTH** • Intellectual development of children ages 7 to 12 improves steadily, allowing them to become capable of new ways of thinking.
• Jean Piaget	**THEORIES ABOUT HOW CHILDREN LEARN** • Piaget's concrete operations stage includes: classifying objects, extending relationships, placing objects in a series, and conservation.

Summary

As children grow from ages 7 to 12, brain development continues to increase their ability to learn.

Chapter 18 Intellectual Development from Seven to Twelve

Section 18.1 Brain Development from Seven to Twelve

Mathematics
Placing Objects in a Series

> **NCTM Algebra** Understand patterns, relations, and functions.

Directions Imagine that you are teaching a group of seven-year-olds a lesson on placing objects in a series. The children are to line up different wooden blocks in size order from smallest to largest. Write your lesson based on four of Howard Gardner's intelligences.

_____

_____

_____

_____

_____

_____

_____

_____

_____

_____

_____

_____

_____

_____

_____

_____

_____

_____

Chapter 18 Intellectual Development from Seven to Twelve

Section 18.1 Brain Development from Seven to Twelve

 Study Skills
Improving Concentration

Directions Use the following tips to help improve your concentration. Then review Section 18.1, using the tips to answer the questions. If the statement is true, circle the letter T. If the statement is false, circle the letter F and rewrite the statement so it is true.

Improving Concentration
• Remove distractions such as telephones and televisions from your study area.
• Take a break every 20 minutes.
• As you are studying, remind yourself to think about what you are reading.

1. Most children begin to move into Piaget's concrete operations   T / F
   stage at about age eleven. _____
   _____

2. During Piaget's formal operations stage, children develop the   T / F
   ability to think abstractly and to see different sides of an issue.
   _____

3. Vygotsky's theory says that biological development and cultural   T / F
   experience both influence children's ability to learn. _____
   _____

4. Montessori stressed the importance of teacher-directed   T / F
   learning. _____
   _____

5. Gardner, who proposed the theory of multiple intelligences,   T / F
   challenged Piaget by theorizing that knowledge is multifaceted.
   _____

6. Sternberg's theory proposes that people have varying degrees   T / F
   of analytical, creative, and practical intelligence. _____
   _____

Chapter 18

Chapter 18 Intellectual Development from Seven to Twelve

Section 18.2 Learning from Seven to Twelve

 Note Taking

Directions As you read, write notes, facts, and main ideas in the Note Taking column. Write key words and short phrases in the Cues column. Then summarize the section in the Summary box.

Cues	Note Taking
• learning methods	**LEARNING METHODS** • Seven- to 12-year-olds become more capable of abstract thought and of more demanding work.
• new independence	**MIDDLE SCHOOL—A TIME OF TRANSITION** • Students become more aware of their own bodies and are looking for peer acceptance.
• standardized tests	**INTELLECTUAL DEVELOPMENT** • Schools regularly give standardized tests.

Summary
Young children learn skills mainly through imitating older children and adults.

Chapter 18

Chapter 18 Intellectual Development from Seven to Twelve

Section 18.2 Learning from Seven to Twelve

 Social Studies
Middle School Transitions

NCSS IV H Individual Development and Indentity Work independently and cooperatively within groups and institutions to accomplish goals.

Directions Work with a partner to write a two- to three-minute script about one of the transitions that middle schoolers go through. Be prepared to share your script with the rest of the class.

_____

_____

_____

_____

_____

_____

_____

_____

_____

_____

_____

_____

_____

_____

_____

_____

_____

_____

_____

_____

_____

_____

_____

_____

_____

Chapter 18

Name _____ Date _____ Class _____

Chapter 18 Intellectual Development from Seven to Twelve

Section 18.2 Learning from Seven to Twelve

 Test Prep
Using Quotations in Essay Tests

Directions Read the information on using quotations in essay tests. Then write a short essay using all or part of the list of quotations taken from your textbook.

Using Quotations in Essay Tests
• Quotations can lend credibility to your essay-test answer. Use quotations from an authority to make your point. • Quotations can be very short. Three or four words are often sufficient. • Instead of using a direct quotation, a reference to it also can be effective. • When you include a quotation in your essay, be sure to attribute it in the essay, or cite the source of the quotation. • Use quotations selectively. Overuse of quotations will distract from your essay answer.

List of Quotations from Your Textbook

"The brain is the center of learning."

"Memory is central to all learning."

"Improvements in the way the brain functions allow older children and preteens to learn more and to use their knowledge more efficiently."

_____

_____

_____

_____

_____

_____

_____

_____

_____

_____

_____

Chapter 18

Chapter 18 Intellectual Development from Seven to Twelve

Chapter Vocabulary

English Language Arts
Writing Essays

NCTE 12 Use language to accomplish individual purposes.

Directions Use all of these vocabulary terms in a short essay. Be sure to proofread your essay and correct any grammar or spelling errors.

- transitivity
- conservation
- hypothetical
- learning method
- peer learning

- standardized test
- concrete
- multifaceted
- integrate
- mandate

_____
_____
_____
_____
_____
_____
_____
_____
_____
_____
_____
_____
_____
_____
_____
_____
_____
_____
_____
_____

Chapter 18

Chapter 19   Adolescence
Section 19.1 Physical Development of Adolescents

 Note Taking

Directions As you read, write notes, facts, and main ideas in the Note
Taking column. Write key words and short phrases in the Cues column.
Then summarize the section in the Summary box.

Cues	Note Taking
• challenges and changes	**PHYSICAL DEVELOPMENT DURING ADOLESCENCE** • Adolescence is the teen years, ages 13 to 19.
• balanced diet	**HEALTH AND WELLNESS** • Puberty and growth spurts impact teens' nutritional needs.

Summary
Generally, adolescence refers to the complex time of life when a child begins to mature into an adult.

Chapter 19

Chapter 19 Adolescence

Section 19.1 Physical Development of Adolescents

 Science
Weekly Activity Schedule

Directions Use the chart to plan one week of moderate to vigorous physical activities appropriate for adolescents. Activities should last at least 60 minutes. You can plan for more than one activity during the 60-minute period.

One-Week Activity Schedule	
Day	**Activity**
Monday	
Tuesday	
Wednesday	
Thursday	
Friday	
Saturday	
Sunday	

Chapter 19 Adolescence
Section 19.1 Physical Development of Adolescents

 Study Skills
Learning New Material

Directions Read the tips for learning new material. Then answer the questions on Section 19.1.

Learning New Material
• Preview the material by scanning the table of contents, headings, and captions. • Break up the material into smaller parts. • After reading a section, explain the information in your own words, as if you were teaching someone else. • Reread any parts that are not clear to you.

1. Scan section 19.1. Explain how the section is structured.

_____

_____

_____

2. How would you break up Section 19.1 to make it easier to read?

_____

_____

_____

3. Read Section 19.1 again. Write a short summary of each smaller part you created in question 2.

_____

_____

_____

4. Did this study strategy help you better comprehend what you read in this section? Why or why not?

_____

_____

_____

Chapter 19

Chapter 19 Adolescence

Section 19.2 Emotional, Social, and Moral Development of Adolescents

 Note Taking

Directions As you read, write notes, facts, and main ideas in the Note Taking column. Write key words and short phrases in the Cues column. Then summarize the section in the Summary box.

Cues	Note Taking
• personal identity	**EMOTIONAL DEVELOPMENT OF ADOLESCENTS** • Teens strive to establish personal identities.
• peer groups	**SOCIAL RELATIONSHIPS IN ADOLESCENCE** • Peers play an important role in teens' social development.
• morality	**MORAL DEVELOPMENT OF ADOLESCENTS** • Moral development guides teens' behavior as it gives them a greater awareness of the rules of society.

Summary
Adolescence is often a time of confusion, but it can also lead to a strong sense of self.

Chapter 19 Adolescence
Section 19.2 Emotional, Social, and Moral Development
of Adolescents

Social Studies
Affecting Personal Identity

NCSS IV A Individual Development and Identity Articulate personal connections to time, place, and social/cultural system.

Directions Write a personal narrative on a separate sheet of paper in which you explain how family, peers, the media, and your hopes for the future have affected the formation of your personal identity. Review the tips for writing narratives. Use the space to organize your thoughts before you begin the narrative.

Tips on Writing Narratives

- Test your ideas by talking them through or by free-writing.
- Ask yourself questions to fill out details of the narrative.
- Construct a time line or other graphic organizer for your narrative.
- Proofread for grammar and spelling errors.

_____

_____

_____

_____

_____

_____

_____

_____

_____

_____

_____

_____

_____

_____

_____

_____

Chapter 19

Chapter 19 Adolescence

Section 19.2 Emotional, Social, and Moral Development of Adolescents

 Test Prep
Coping with Test Anxiety

Directions Practice these tips for decreasing anxiety before and during tests. Then answer the questions.

Tips to Decrease Test Anxiety
• Remember that this is only one test. It may be an important one, but it is not the only test on which your grade depends.
• When you get jittery, take a deep breath. Count slowly to three while you inhale.
• Get plenty of rest the night before the test.

1. What social and cultural influences affect a teen's formation of a personal identity?

_____

_____

2. How can parents and teachers help prevent serious emotional difficulties in teens?

_____

_____

3. List some warning signs of depression.

_____

_____

4. Discuss two sources of tension between teens and their families.

_____

_____

5. Why should parents not worry too much about their teen's conformist behavior?

_____

_____

6. Why is it important to have a best friend during adolescence?

_____

Chapter 19

Chapter 19 Adolescence
Section 19.3 Intellectual Development of Adolescents
 Note Taking

Directions As you read, write notes, facts, and main ideas in the Note Taking column. Write key words and short phrases in the Cues column. Then summarize the section in the Summary box.

Cues	Note Taking
• brain growth	**BRAIN DEVELOPMENT IN ADOLESCENTS** • Teens gain the ability to think in more complex and sophisticated ways.
• abstract thinking	**TEEN INTELLECTUAL DEVELOPMENT** • Adolescents reach Piaget's fourth stage, the period of formal operations.

Summary

Dramatic advances in brain development come with the physical and emotional changes of the adolescent years.

Chapter 19

Chapter 19 Adolescence

Section 19.3 Intellectual Development of Adolescents

English Language Arts
Write a Persuasive Paper

NCTE 1 Read texts to acquire new information.

Directions Re-read the information in Section 19.3 about Piaget's and Vygotsky's theories. Then use the library or Internet to do additional research on their theories. After you have completed your research, choose either Piaget's or Vygotsky's theory and write a persuasive paper in which you argue in favor of the theory you have chosen. Use these tips as you write your argument.

Tips for Writing a Persuasive Paper

- State your position clearly
- Use facts to back up your position

_____

_____

_____

_____

_____

_____

_____

_____

_____

_____

_____

_____

_____

_____

_____

_____

_____

_____

Chapter 19 Adolescence
Chapter Vocabulary

 English Language Arts
Writing Sentences

Directions Choose four of the vocabulary terms. Find each term in the text and copy one sentence here. Then rewrite the sentences in your own words to demonstrate your understanding of the terms.

Content Vocabulary

- testosterone
- estrogen
- personal identity
- identity crisis

- depression
- bipolar disorder
- morality
- moral maturity

- popular culture
- prefrontal cortex
- amygdala
- abstract thought

---

1. Sentence from text: Testosterone levels in a boy's body begin to rise rapidly at the beginning of puberty.

   Rewritten sentence: During puberty, a boy's body produces more of the hormone, testosterone.

2. Sentence from text: _____

   _____

   Rewritten sentence: _____

   _____

3. Sentence from text: _____

   _____

   Rewritten sentence: _____

   _____

4. Sentence from text: _____

   _____

   Rewritten sentence: _____

   _____

Chapter 20 Children's Health and Safety

Section 20.1 Childhood Illnesses

 Note Taking

Directions As you read, write notes, facts, and main ideas in the Note Taking column. Write key words and short phrases in the Cues column. Then summarize the section in the Summary box.

Cues	Note Taking
• regular examinations	**REGULAR CHECKUPS** • Early detection of a child's medical problems and follow-up treatment may prevent a minor condition from becoming serious.
• symptoms of illnesses	**CARING FOR A SICK CHILD** • All children get sick at times.

Summary
Children should have regular medical checkups.

Chapter 20

Chapter 20 Children's Health and Safety
Section 20.1 Childhood Illnesses

Science
Pocket Guide to Childhood Illnesses

NSES F Students should develop understanding of personal and community health.

Directions Use information in Section 20.1 to create a pocket guide to childhood illnesses. Your guide should include the names of common childhood illnesses, the symptoms parents and caregivers should be able to recognize, and the treatments for the illnesses. Make your pocket guide attractive and easy to use. Use the space to organize your thoughts before you create your guide.

_____

_____

_____

_____

_____

_____

_____

_____

_____

_____

_____

_____

_____

_____

_____

_____

_____

_____

Chapter 20

Chapter 20 Children's Health and Safety
Section 20.1 Childhood Illnesses

Study Skills
Make Connections

Directions Making personal connections to the content of this chapter can help you better understand the information. For instance, it is likely that you suffered a childhood illness at some point in your life. You might have even experienced a hospital stay. Use such personal experiences to answer these questions so that you might better relate to a child who has an illness.

1. Describe your illness. _____

_____

_____

_____

2. Explain how the illness was diagnosed and treated. _____

_____

_____

_____

3. Share your feelings during this time in your life. _____

_____

_____

_____

4. Explain how this experience might help you understand and relate to a sick child. _____

_____

_____

_____

Name _____ Date _____ Class _____

Chapter 20 Children's Health and Safety
Section 20.2 Accidents and Emergencies

 Note Taking

Directions As you read, write notes, facts, and main ideas in the Note Taking column. Write key words and short phrases in the Cues column. Then summarize the section in the Summary box.

Cues	Note Taking
• different ages, different hazards	**SAFETY** • To keep children safe, caregivers must know what to expect in any situation.
• bleeding	**FIRST AID** • The American Red Cross can provide information about first aid training classes.
• rescue breathing	**RESCUE TECHNIQUES** • Immediate and correct action is required when a child stops breathing or his heart stops beating.

Summary

A caregiver's most important responsibility is to keep children safe.

Chapter 20 Children's Health and Safety
Section 20.2 Accidents and Emergencies

 English Language Arts
Emergency Guidelines Brochure

> **NCTE 4** Use written language
> to communicate effectively.

Directions Use information from Section 20.2 to create a brochure of
emergency guidelines. Your brochure should have three sections: Safety,
First Aid, and Rescue Techniques. Do not overcrowd the brochure, but
be sure to include all important information. If possible, illustrate the
panels. Use the space below to plan your format.

1 Left Inside Panel	2 Middle Inside Panel	3 Right Inside Panel

4 Inside Flap	5 Back Panel	6 Front Cover

Chapter 20 Children's Health and Safety

Section 20.2 Accidents and Emergencies

 **Test Prep**
Reviewing Strategies

Directions Read the reviewing strategies. Then answer the questions.

Reviewing Strategies
• Create a study checklist for all the material on which you will be tested. Use your notes, text assignments, handouts, and past quizzes and tests. • Use the checklist to break the review material into smaller chunks. • Create a visual image, such as a concept map of the important ideas and their relationships to each other. • Make an audio recording of the important notes and listen to it while you take walks.

1. How do you treat a child's nosebleed?

   _____

   _____

   _____

2. Why should you wear disposable gloves when giving first aid to a bleeding child?

   _____

   _____

   _____

3. In what cases should you seek medical attention for a cut?

   _____

   _____

   _____

4. In what circumstances would you seek medical help for a splinter?

   _____

   _____

   _____

Chapter 20

Chapter 20 Children's Health and Safety

Chapter Vocabulary

 English Language Arts
Matching Definitions

NCTE 12 Use language
to accomplish individual
purposes.

Directions Match each word to its definition by
writing the letter that corresponds to the word before the sentence that
defines it.

a. communicable disease
b. pollen
c. asthma
d. contagious
e. antiseptic
f. fracture
g. sprain

h. abdominal thrust
i. convulsion
j. hives
k. shock
l. rescue breathing
m. cardiopulmonary resuscitation
   (CPR)

_____l_____ **1.** a procedure for forcing air into the lungs of a person who is not
breathing

_____ **2.** a brief period during which muscles suddenly contract, causing the person to fall and twitch or jerk; also known as a seizure

_____ **3.** a disease that is passed from one person to another

_____ **4.** a condition that causes the lungs to contract more than they should, narrowing the air passages and making it difficult to breathe

_____ **5.** a quick upward thrust with the heel of the hand into the abdomen that
forces the air in the lungs to expel an object caught in the throat

_____ **6.** combines rescue breathing with chest compressions to restore breathing
and circulation

_____ **7.** the person with the illness can pass it on to someone else

_____ **8.** a break or crack in a bone

_____ **9.** blisterlike sores caused by an allergic reaction

_____ **10.** powder-like grains that come from seed plants

_____ **11.** an injury caused by sudden, violent stretching of a joint or muscle

_____ **12.** a serious medical condition in which important body functions, including breathing and heartbeat, are impaired

_____ **13.** a substance that prevents or stops the growth of germs

Chapter 20

Chapter 21 Family Challenges
Section 21.1 Family Stresses

 Note Taking

Directions As you read, write notes, facts, and main ideas in the Note Taking column. Write key words and short phrases in the Cues column. Then summarize the section in the Summary box.

Cues	Note Taking
• children are vulnerable	**CHILDREN AND STRESS** • Parents can help children cope with stress by listening patiently and accepting their feelings of anger, grief, and sadness.
• situational stress	**CAUSES OF STRESS** • Situational stress comes from the environment or certain circumstances and changes.

Summary
Because of their lack of understanding, children can often be more susceptible to stress than adults.

Chapter 21 Family Challenges

Section 21.1 Family Stresses

 Mathematics
Calculate Percentages

> **NCTM Problem Solving** Apply and adapt a variety of appropriate strategies to solve problems.

Directions Families that experience financial crises sometimes face homelessness. Homelessness can be extremely stressful for all family members. Conduct research using trusted resources to fill in the table. Get the most current information you can on how many families live in your city, town, or county; your state; and the United States. Then find how many families in each of these areas are homeless. Calculate these numbers as percentages.

Homelessness Statistics

Categories	City, Town or County	State	United States
Total number of families			
Number of homeless families			
Percentage of families that are homeless			

Chapter 21 Family Challenges

Section 21.1 Family Stresses

Study Skills
Using Your Own Words

Directions Writing down responses to material you have read can increase your level of understanding. Read the tips for writing paragraphs. Then write one paragraph that describes your thoughts about school and stress.

Writing Good Paragraphs
• A paragraph should contain a topic sentence that delivers the main idea of the paragraph. The topic sentence is often the first sentence in the paragraph.
• The topic sentence should be supported with sentences that clarify the topic and provide meaningful details.
• Vary the length of the sentences. This will make the paragraph more interesting and easier to read.
• Delete unnecessary words that might distract the reader from the paragraph's main idea.

_____

_____

_____

_____

_____

_____

_____

_____

_____

_____

_____

_____

_____

Chapter 21

Chapter 21 Family Challenges

Section 21.2 Children with Special Needs

 Note Taking

Directions As you read, write notes, facts, and main ideas in the Note Taking column. Write key words and short phrases in the Cues column. Then summarize the section in the Summary box.

Cues	Note Taking
• learning disabilities	**CHILDREN WITH DISABILITIES** • Some disabilities are evident at birth. Some are not discovered for months or years.
• special abilities	**GIFTED CHILDREN** • Gifted children show, or show potential for, special abilities in one or more areas.

Summary
Children with special needs have different needs from the average child.

Chapter 21 Family Challenges
Section 21.2 Children with Special Needs

Science
Finding Gifted Students

NSES A Students should develop abilities necessary to do scientific inquiry, understandings about scientific inquiry.

Directions Interview a counselor at a local elementary, middle, and high school to find the total number of students enrolled at their school and the total number of gifted students who attend. Then calculate the percentage of gifted students at each school. Ask each counselor what kind of program is available for their school's gifted students. Use the information you gathered to fill in the table and describe the programs.

Gifted Students Statistics			
	Total School Enrollment	Total Number of Gifted Students	Percentage of Gifted Students Enrolled
Elementary school			
Middle school			
High school			

Programs Available for Gifted Students

Elementary school: _____

_____

_____

Middle school: _____

_____

_____

High school: _____

_____

_____

Chapter 21 Family Challenges

Section 21.2 Children with Special Needs

 Test Prep
Taking Tests

Directions Read the tips for taking tests. Then answer the questions by circling the letter next to the correct answer.

Test Taking Tips
• Read over the test directions and underline words that will help you follow directions, such as "summarize", "compare and contrast", or "explain your answer." • When you have completed the test, make sure you answered every question. • Re-read your answers for essay and short-answer questions. Check the spelling, grammar, and sentence structure.

1. Disabilities may result from difficulties with
   a. mobility.
   b. vision.
   c. hearing.
   d. all of the above.

2. Dyslexia is a common learning disability that prevents a child from
   a. staying in his or her seat to complete a task.
   b. pronouncing words correctly.
   c. understanding printed symbols in a normal way.
   d. hearing and understanding verbal instructions.

3. Down syndrome is an example of a genetic disorder resulting in varying degrees of
   a. ADHD.
   b. ADD.
   c. autism.
   d. mental retardation.

4. Developmental delays, mental retardation, and physical abnormalities are characteristics of
   a. asthma.
   b. hyperactivity.
   c. fetal alcohol syndrome.
   d. type 1 diabetes.

5. The federal law that ensures that children with disabilities receive a free public education that meets their needs is called
   a. ADHD.
   b. IEP.
   c. IDEA.
   d. ADD.

6. Children who show special abilities in one or more areas are called
   a. geniuses.
   b. autistic.
   c. disabled.
   d. gifted.

Chapter 21 Family Challenges
Section 21.3 Child Abuse and Neglect

 Note Taking

Directions As you read, write notes, facts, and main ideas in the Note Taking column. Write key words and short phrases in the Cues column. Then summarize the section in the Summary box.

Cues	Note Taking
• types of maltreatment	**MALTREATMENT** • Most incidents of child abuse never come to the attention of authorities.
• at-risk children	**WHY DOES ABUSE OCCUR?** • Some children, such as those with physical or mental disabilities and younger children, are more at risk of being abused.
• waiting to have children	**STOP MALTREATMENT** • Parenting classes can help people learn skills for raising children.

Summary

Hundreds of thousands of children become victims of child abuse and neglect each year, often at the hands of their parents.

Chapter 21

Chapter 21 Family Challenges
Section 21.3 Child Abuse and Neglect

 English Language Arts
Effects of Long-Term Abuse

NCTE 7 Conduct research and gather, evaluate, and synthesize data to communicate discoveries.

Directions Use library and Internet resources to conduct research about the long-term effects of abuse. Find information about the effects of abuse 5, 10, 15, or more years after its occurrence. How have the victims coped? Have they become productive citizens? Do they have emotional issues? Have they become abusers? Report your findings.

Choose one of these topics as the focus for your research:
- physical abuse
- neglect
- sexual abuse
- emotional and verbal abuse

Use the rest of this page to plan your report.

_____

_____

_____

_____

_____

_____

_____

_____

_____

_____

_____

_____

_____

_____

_____

Chapter 21 Family Challenges

Chapter Vocabulary

 English Language Arts
Fill in the Blanks

NCTE 12 Use language to accomplish individual purposes.

Directions Fill in the blank with the correct Content Vocabulary term. You will not use all of the terms.

Content Vocabulary

- ADD
- addiction
- addiction counselor
- ADHD
- asthma
- autism
- autism spectrum disorder (ASD)
- crisis nursery
- dyslexia

- gifted
- inclusion
- learning disability
- mandated reporter
- mental retardation
- regression
- situational stress
- support group
- type 1 diabetes

---

1. A ___crisis nursery___ is a child care facility where troubled parents can go to receive short-term, free child care.

2. _____ is the temporary backward movement to an earlier stage of development.

3. A therapist trained to help substance abusers is called an _____.

4. A _____ interferes with a child's ability to learn, listen, think, speak, read, write, spell, or do math.

5. _____ is stress that comes from the environment a child lives in or from certain circumstances and changes

6. _____ is one of a group of disorders collectively known as

   _____.

7. A person who is required by law to report maltreatment is a _____.

8. Children with _____ have below-average intelligence and skills.

9. A _____ is a collection of individuals who work together to explore and accept their feelings.

10. An _____ is a dependence on a substance such as alcohol or drugs.

11. _____ means placing children with disabilities in regular classrooms while they also receive special education services.

Chapter 22 Child Care and Early Education
Section 22.1 Child Care Options

 Note Taking

Directions As you read, write notes, facts, and main ideas in the Note Taking column. Write key words and short phrases in the Cues column. Then summarize the section in the Summary box.

Cues	Note Taking
• home-based care	**SUBSTITUTE CARE** • There are many types of substitute child care.
• quality of care	**CHOOSING SUBSTITUTE CHILD CARE** • Many factors must be considered when choosing substitute child care.

Summary
Many parents rely on other people to care for their children at least some of the time.

Chapter 22

Chapter 22 Child Care and Early Education
Section 22.1 Child Care Options

Social Studies
Choosing Child Care

> **NCSS I A Culture** Analyze and explain the ways groups, societies, and cultures address human needs and concerns.

Directions Follow your teacher's directions to form groups. Work with the members of your group to identify and write questions to ask when choosing home- or center-based child care. Question topics might include: references, licensing, accreditation, child-to-staff ratio, cost, or backup plans. Then contact a home- or center-based care center to get answers to your questions. Use this page to help plan your questions.

QUESTIONS FOR CHOOSING CHILD CARE

Question: _____

Answer: _____

Question: _____

Answer: _____

Question: _____

Answer: _____

Question: _____

Answer: _____

Question: _____

Answer: _____

Question: _____

Answer: _____

Question: _____

Answer: _____

Chapter 22

Chapter 22 Child Care and Early Education
Section 22.1 Child Care Options

Study Skills
Taking Notes During Class

Directions Use these guidelines to improve your in-class note-taking skills. Use your notes to answer the questions.

Taking Notes During Class
• Listen actively. • Be open-minded about the points that your teacher makes. Do not dwell on them. Focus on taking notes. • Develop and use a standard method of note taking, such as punctuating, abbreviating, and writing in margins. • Take and keep notes in a large notebook. • Leave a few blank spaces as you move from one point to the next so you can fill in additional points later.

1. ___Accreditation___ means that the child care provider has met strict official standards for quality child care.

2. _____ takes place in the caregiver's home.

3. A _____ is child care that is provided by the parents of the children in the cooperative.

4. A _____ is an arrangement in which parents take turns caring for one another's children in their own homes.

5. A _____ is a registration with the state that indicates child care providers meet health and safety standards.

6. A _____ is a facility in which a staff of adults provides care for children.

7. _____ is a program that provides locally run child care facilities designed to help lower-income and disadvantaged children from birth to age five become ready for school.

8. A _____ is a person trained to provide child care.

9. _____ is provided to many young children from a caregiver who comes to their home.

10. While quality of care is the primary consideration in choosing child care, _____ is also an important factor.

Chapter 22 Child Care and Early Education
Section 22.2 Participating in Early Childhood Education

 Note Taking

Directions As you read, write notes, facts, and main ideas in the Note Taking column. Write key words and short phrases in the Cues column. Then summarize the section in the Summary box.

Cues	Note Taking
• carefully designed environment	**THE EARLY CHILDHOOD CLASSROOM** • The environment in early childhood classrooms must be child-size to promote children's independence.
• learning through play	**PLANNING APPROPRIATE ACTIVITIES** • The daily schedule should provide a variety of activities.
• setting expectations	**PROMOTING POSITIVE BEHAVIOR** • Teachers must communicate expectations to children and model good behavior.

Summary
Early childhood classrooms are carefully designed to meet children's varied needs.

Chapter 22

Chapter 22 Child Care and Early Education

Section 22.2 Participating in Early Childhood Education

 Science
Health Care Routines

| NSES F Students should develop understanding of personal and community health. |

Directions Create a poster of health care routines that could be used in a child care facility to prevent the spread of illness. Make your poster bright and colorful, and include a title and illustrations. Use this page to plan and design your poster.

Chapter 22

Chapter 22 Child Care and Early Education
Section 22.2 Participating in Early Childhood Education

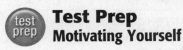 **Test Prep**
Motivating Yourself

Directions Read the tips on motivating yourself. Then fill in information on starting up your own child care magazine for parents.

Motivating Yourself
• Instead of studying because you have to, focus on why you want to learn the material. For example, you may want to know more about the subject, get an A in the class, or learn enough to pass the test. • Brainstorm and make a list of the reasons you want to pass the test. Write down as many reasons as you can. • Visualize the reward you will receive for passing the test.

1. Describe the type of information you will provide in your magazine.

   _____

   _____

   _____

   _____

2. Describe your targeted audience.

   _____

   _____

   _____

   _____

3. What will be your criteria for allowing companies to advertise in your magazine?

   _____

   _____

   _____

   _____

Chapter 22 Child Care and Early Education
Chapter Vocabulary

English Language Arts
Writing Sentences

NCTE 12 Use language to accomplish individual purposes.

Directions Use 10 of the Content Vocabulary terms in original sentences that show you understand their meaning.

Copyright © by The McGraw-Hill Companies, Inc. All rights reserved.

Content Vocabulary

- child care center
- in-home care
- family child care
- nanny
- license
- accreditation
- play group
- parent cooperative
- Head Start
- learning center
- circle time
- free play
- transition

---

1. _____

_____

2. _____

_____

3. _____

_____

4. _____

_____

5. _____

_____

6. _____

_____

7. _____

_____

8. _____

9. _____

_____

Chapter 23 Careers Working with Children
Section 23.1 Preparing for a Career

 Note Taking

Directions As you read, write notes, facts, and main ideas in the Note Taking column. Write key words and short phrases in the Cues column. Then summarize the section in the Summary box.

Cues	Note Taking
• levels of jobs	**CAREER OPTIONS** • Choosing a career path may be difficult.
• tasks and responsibilities	**EVALUATE CAREERS** • There are many factors that must be considered when choosing a career.
• short-term goals	**SETTING AND ACHIEVING GOALS** • Establishing career goals can help you achieve a career that is satisfying, challenging, and worthwhile.

Summary
Most people begin their career search by choosing a career area or career field.

Chapter 23

Chapter 23 Careers Working with Children
Section 23.1 Preparing for a Career

 English Language Arts
Service Learning

> **NCTE 12** Use language to accomplish individual purposes.

Directions Service learning projects get young people involved in their communities. The projects can range from cleaning up a vacant lot to holding a fund-raiser for the family of a child who needs a transplant. Here are some ideas for creating a service learning project:

• Find a need within your community.
• Determine whether you and your classmates can do something to help meet the need.
• Analyze what resources you will need and where you will get them.

Write a service learning project for you and your class to complete. After you have created your project, share it with the class and ask for input.

_____

_____

_____

_____

_____

_____

_____

_____

_____

_____

_____

_____

_____

_____

_____

Chapter 23 Careers Working with Children
Section 23.1 Preparing for a Career

 Study Skills
Short-Term Scheduling

Directions Making schedules is an important part of many jobs. Read about short-term scheduling. Then follow the example and make your own schedule for the next day.

Short-Term Scheduling
One way of keeping track of time and staying on task is to make a schedule for the day. Use a small note card to develop a daily schedule. Specify what you are going to accomplish. Carry this card with you and cross out each item as you accomplish it. Writing down things in this way helps you plan your time, and you also make a promise to yourself to do what you intend to do.

Example

Wednesday
8:00 a.m. – 8:50 a.m. Review history 9:00 a.m. – 3:00 p.m. School
3:00 p.m. – 4:00 p.m. Attend band practice 4:30 p.m. – 5:30 p.m. Attend soccer practice
6:00 p.m. – 7:00 p.m. Dinner 7:00 p.m. – 8:00 p.m. Study chapters 5 and 6 (history)
8:00 p.m. – 8:20 p.m. Break 8:20 p.m. – 9:00 p.m. Study Ch. 4 (child development) and Lesson 3 (Spanish)

Your Schedule

Chapter 23 Careers Working with Children

Section 23.2 Beginning Your Career

Note Taking

Directions As you read, write notes, facts, and main ideas in the Note Taking column. Write key words and short phrases in the Cues column. Then summarize the section in the Summary box.

Cues	Note Taking
• networking	**LOOK FOR A JOB** • Six steps to job hunting include: finding an opening, preparing a résumé, filling out an application, interviewing, following up, and evaluating a job offer.
• job-specific skills	**BUILD CAREER SKILLS** • Job-specific skills are the skills or abilities needed to do a specific job.
• reference	**LEAVING A JOB** • Make every effort to leave your job on good terms.

Summary
Most people must devote a lot of time and effort to finding a job.

Chapter 23 Careers Working with Children
Section 23.2 Beginning Your Career

Mathematics
Calculate Pay

NCTM Number and Operations Compute fluently and make reasonable estimates.

Directions Salary and benefits are often the reasons people choose one job offer over another. Contact three different employers that offer similar jobs. For example, three different schools offer jobs for beginning teachers. Ask about the starting salary. Make sure to write out a phone script before you make your calls. Fill in the table with the information you find. Note: If you are given monthly salary information, you will need to compute how that amount breaks down hourly and weekly, and what it amounts to annually. For computing purposes, use 40 hours per week, 4 weeks per month, and 52 weeks per year.

Telephone script: _____

_____

_____

_____

Entry-Level Salaries			
	Employer #1	Employer #2	Employer #3
Job			
Hourly salary			
Weekly salary			
Monthly salary			
Yearly salary			

Chapter 23

Chapter 23 Careers Working with Children
Section 23.2 Beginning Your Career

test prep **Test Prep**
Questions to Ask About the Test

Directions Read the questions to ask about the test. Then answer the questions by circling **T** if the statement is true or **F** if the statement is false.

Questions to Ask About the Test
Before the day of the test, ask these questions: • What material will be covered on the test? • What kinds of questions will be asked—essay, multiple choice, true/false, or short answer? • How long will I have to complete the test? • Will the test be on the computer or in printed form? • Will the test be open- or closed-book? • How much will this test count toward my grade for this class?

1. The practice of using personal and professional contacts to further your career goals is called a job fair. **T / (F)**

2. A key to a successful job search is organization. **T / F**

3. A cover letter should highlight relevant talents and skills. **T / F**

4. A network is an event where employers with current or future job openings meet with potential employees. **T / F**

5. Most employers do not ask applicants to fill out an application. **T / F**

6. It is important to dress appropriately for a job interview. **T / F**

7. A common question at a job interview is: What are your religious beliefs? **T / F**

8. Flexibility and willingness to change are not important after you have landed a job. **T / F**

9. Being ethical means doing the right thing. **T / F**

10. Transferable skills are needed for any career you choose. **T / F**

Chapter 23 Careers Working with Children

Chapter Vocabulary

 English Language Arts
Graphic Organizers

NCTE 12 Use language to accomplish individual purposes.

Directions Follow the steps to fill in the graphic organizer.

1. Read the terms in the first column.
2. Write what you think the terms mean in the second column.
3. Use a dictionary to learn the definitions of the terms and write them in the third column.

Term	Predict what the term means	Write the dictionary definition
job shadowing	staying in a person's shadow while they are on the job	Observing someone in his or her job
internship		
service learning		
work-based learning		
career path		
career ladder		
networking		
job fair		
résumé		
cover letter		

Chapter 23